Rich and Free

The Entrepreneur's Guide to Creating Wealth and Personal Freedom

Brian J. Bieler

Author of *Powerful Steps-10 Essential Career Skills and Business Strategies for the Workplace Warrior*

**Also By
Brian J. Bieler**

*Powerful Steps: 10 Essential Career Skills and
Business Strategies for the Workplace Warrior*

This book is not intended to provide personalized legal, accounting, financial, or investment advice. Readers are encouraged to seek the counsel of competent professionals with regard to matters as interpretation of the law, proper accounting procedures, tax planning, financial planning, and investment strategies. Laws and practices may vary from state to state and if legal or other assistance is required, the services of a professional should be sought. The Author and Publisher specifically disclaim any liability, loss, or risk, which is incurred as a consequence, directly or indirectly, of the use and application of any of the contents of this work.

Managing, building, improving, investing in a business or career is demanding and people should expect to invest considerable time and effort. You are urged to read all the available material, learn as much as possible about business, investing, and careers, and tailor the information to your individual needs.

Every effort has been made to make this book as complete and accurate as possible. However, there *may be mistakes*, both typographical and in content. Therefore, this text should be used only as a general guide and not as the ultimate source of information. Furthermore, this book contains information that is current only up to the printing date.

Rich and Free
The Entrepreneur's Guide to
Creating Wealth and Personal Freedom

Copyright © 2007 by Brian J. Bieler

Published By:
Little Falls Press
7000 North 16th Street, Suite 120 # 489
Phoenix, AZ 85020-5547

1-800-980-5099

richandfree@cox.net

Visit our website at:
www.richandfreeguide.com

Unattributed quotations are by Brian J. Bieler

ISBN-10: 0-9779569-3-8
ISBN-13: 978-0-9779569-3-7

Cover design by

Blue Bus Media
Los Angeles, CA 310-985-5165
www.bluebusmedia.com

Acknowledgements

My wife Ann plays a special part and helps keep me focused and energized, I could not do this work without her and am thankful for her support. My children Drew and Danielle cheer me on and my son Jeff takes a special interest and helps with ideas and editing. And thanks to Lisa my daughter-in-law for her creative input and time.

I want to thank the accomplished people that have given me input and great ideas, no one has a corner on creating success and riches. The feedback from entrepreneurs and millionaires that have done it through perspiration, wit, wisdom, smart strategies and taking risks have helped me stay on track.

My sincere thanks and acknowledgement to the following friends, new and old, who have helped and contributed to this book. If you helped in any way and are not on this list, please pardon our oversight and know that we thank you as well.

Many thanks to Charlie Colombo, Executive VP United Stations; Bernadette Duncan, Launch Radio Networks Talk Satellite; Courtney R. Thompson, CEO Thompson Management & Marketing; Mike "Murph" Murphy, owner and broadcast entrepreneur; Diane Kennedy, C.P.A. *New York Times* best selling author *Loop-Holes of the Rich*; James A. Ziegler, CSP National Speakers Association author *The Prosperity Equation*; Ed Gargano, CEO Gargano Communications; Nancy Cole, publisher *The Equestrian News* Los Angeles; Thomas Mooney, Clear Channel Radio Regional Controller; Jim M. Allen, The Big Idea Coach™;

Flo Herald, Herald, Inc.; DC Cordova, CEO/Co-founder Excellerated Business Schools®; Janelle L. Etchepare, Hotel Sales/Marketing Manager Enterprise Rent a Car Los Angeles; Doug Setter, author and Bachelor Human Ecology; Rebecca Jacoby, copywriter and ghostwriter; Jeff Holden, Regional Market Manager Clear Channel Radio; Bob Hughes, Chairman/CEO Compass Radio; Caroline W. Melberg, Founder of Small Business Mavericks and author of *Local Small Business Internet Marketing Secrets*; Marilyn J. Eellez, certified career coach; Marsha A. Johnson, "Harley Girl" author and speaker; "Coach" Gary Micheloni, author and columnist; Stuart Newby, London England entrepreneur and investor; Thom King, Southwest Multimedia Holdings; Mike Wilson, Antananarivo Madagascar CEO Riverstone Minerals; Bob Cole, KVET Radio; Henry Rabyo, Pro Pacific Corp; Michael Monji, author; Mark Waters, CBS Radio Market Manager; Richard R. Blake, Midwest Book Review.

Thank you,

Brian J. Bieler

Dedicated to the Entrepreneur...

Entrepreneurs are the people who take control of their future. They are the innovators and risk takers that give us alternatives and help shape our future.

Table of Contents

Introduction

The man who grasps an opportunity as it is paraded before him, nine times out of ten makes a success, but the man who makes his own opportunities is, barring an accident, a sure-fire success.

—Dale Carnegie

A Lot Has Changed

I took the slow road. I worked twenty-five years before I saw seven figures in my bank account. That is one heck of a lot of meetings, travel, strategic planning sessions, research projects, workshops, seminars, training, hiring, negotiating and weekend work. I never found a get quick rich formula, my career was a slow slug up hill.

However, a lot has changed. You can get rich faster today than any time in history. It's because we work in a bigger connected global marketplace. The new generation has more opportunity in a faster moving economy.

The government allows you to become rich but will do little to *help you get rich*. The system encourages business people with lower taxes and special incentives. You must become financially literate and think like an entrepreneur to take advantage of these opportunities.

Focus on doing what works, not just doing work. People get rich because of desire, specific knowledge, and mastering wealth-creating skills.

Rich and Free is a street-smart guide to help you reach your goals. It's a book of real-life experiences, wealth creating skills and ideas to help you get out of the rat race.

Part 1

It Takes Skills and Knowledge to get Rich and Free

The phrase "red herring" was written about in the *Oxford English Dictionary* in 1686. It described the practice of dragging a smoked herring over a hunted fox trail leaving a strong sent for trained hunting hounds to follow. The dead fish scent was so strong the dogs were distracted from following the scent of the fox, allowing the quarry to escape. And so, the hunt was on.

Money is a red herring, the appearance and smell is distracting. People who follow the scent of money are diverted from the objective. To get money, *you do not go after the money*. You go after the skills and knowledge, which will lead you to the money.

The skills in *Part 1* of *Rich and Free* leverage your ability to get rich. Like the game of golf, you don't get to be a professional because you play the game; you get to be professional because you drill and practice the game.

When you study the wealthy and successful, you find mostly average people but with a high degree of focus, desire, and commitment. Creating wealth and getting rich has little to do with formal education, intelligence or a high IQ. It's about skills and financial literacy. To get rich and independent, learn the skills and thinking of rich and independent people.

Chapter 1

Desire, Commitment and Persistence

It doesn't matter how many times you fail. It doesn't matter how many times you almost get it right. No one is going to know or care about your failures, and neither should you. All you have to do is learn from them and those around you because... All that matters in business is that you get it right once. Then everyone can tell you how lucky you are.

—**Mark Cuban**
Entrepreneur, Innovator, Billionaire
Owner of the Dallas Mavericks

If you are persistent enough, something will happen. Staying the course is what determines the outcome, not how long it takes. If you persist, you can win.

Courage Equals Commitment Plus Doubt

It takes courage to make commitments; no one is immune from doubt. Overcome fears by staying focused. Don't quit at the first sign of things not going your way. Nothing is over until you quit.

Creating wealth is easy to talk about and almost everyone does. However, it's mostly talk, daydreaming and buying lottery tickets. Making a commitment to get rich, that is a different story.

If you put crabs in a bucket, you will not have to worry about them getting out. If any one of them starts to climb out of the bucket, others will pull them back.

If you try to do things others have not been able to achieve, be prepared to have them behave like the crabs. It's a natural response. People who have not been able to achieve riches themselves may be jealous of your trying.

Develop a Thick Skin

Develop a thick skin and don't let negative people influence your thinking. Share your ideas with people who are interested in you and your success.

When you accomplish things, you will have your hands full of people wanting to join you. In the beginning however, don't think everyone will be excited about your ideas unless something is in it for them.

The story that follows is one that I have written about in the past. It is about a black man growing up in the seedy parts of New York. He was determined to be successful and was able to overcome adversity most will never face. Picture yourself in Lee's situation and you people may feel better about your odds of success. It takes courage, commitment, and persistence to withstand years of deprivation.

A Story of Courage and Commitment

Growing up in Brooklyn, New York, Lee Dunham dreamt of being an entrepreneur. He had a shoeshine stand and collected milk bottles while the other kids were out playing. Lee came from a black family of laborers. He would tell his mother, "When I grow up, I want to start my own business." His mom told him time after time, "There's no way you're going to open your own business."

Lee grew up, but never forgot his dream. He joined the Air Force after high school, enrolled in the Air Force food service, and promoted to officer's cook. After the Air Force, he worked for restaurants including the Waldorf Astoria in New York City. He went to night school to sharpen his business skills and applied to the police academy. Lee started a fifteen-year full time career as a beat cop in Harlem's 28th Precinct.

His commitment to own a business never stopped. Lee continued his night classes and worked part time jobs. "I saved every penny I earned as a police officer. For ten years, I didn't spend one dime. No movies, no vacations, no trips to the ballpark." He had one focus, owning a restaurant.

He put restaurant business plans together but he could not be financed. The idea of a "classy tablecloth place" was not going to happen. "Not too many banks willing to lend a lot of money to a black guy in 1971," said Lee. But his dream did not fizzle out. He would find another way and thought about franchising. Lee tried Chicken Delight and others. Finally, he met with McDonald's and they agreed to a franchise but it had to be in the inner city.

No Turning Back

Lee put his life savings of $42,000 on the line and borrowed another $150,000 to start the business. In 1971, Lee opened the first McDonald's franchise in Harlem, New

York. It was a very tough neighborhood and problems started right away.

On opening day kids threw things at Ronald McDonald. They had to bring the clown back to the restaurant for safety. The crowd yelled, "You're not from the neighborhood. You're not a brother. Come back when you're black!" Things continued downhill after the store opened. Street gangs and gunfire scared customers away. Employees stole food, took the cash, and robbed the safe. Lee had to hire his cop friends to keep the gangs out of the restaurant. His confidence was shaken but Lee was not going to quit so easily after years of sacrifice and commitment.

Lee understood poor black people. He knew what they were thinking and how hopeless they felt. He thought of a strategy, came up with a plan, and called the gang members to a meeting.

"I grew up poor, just like all of you," Lee told them. "But I will not allow the restaurant to be a battleground any longer." He challenged them to stop the violence and fighting. It was time to rebuild their lives he said, and convinced the gang members they were only hurting themselves. He offered them jobs and agreed to train them to run a business but only if they worked at the restaurant.

"The only escape of being poor is to work your way out," Lee said. The gang members created goals, learned management skills, and street fighting in front of the restaurant stopped. The Harlem franchise went on to become one of the most profitable in the McDonald's chain earning over $1.5 million dollars a year. Lee was able to rebound and build a restaurant management business. Today he owns restaurants in New York and New Jersey and employees over 500 people.

When people are motivated, they become determined. Motivation may come from having been deprived or raised in hardships.

Many overcome adversity and become stronger. If you have had a challenging life, you may wind up better in the end. People used to adversity are less willing to let obstacles hold them back. They may take on challenges others will not risk.

> *One of the most difficult things everyone has to learn is that for your entire life you must keep fighting and adjusting if you hope to survive. No matter who you are or what your position is you must keep fighting for whatever it is you desire to achieve.*
>
> **—George Allen**

It's How we React

Success comes from how we react to what happens to us. Life is not predictable; success does not go in a straight line. The ability to adjust to surroundings and environment makes us winners. How we think makes us uniquely different and ultimately creates our success.

The power of positive thinking is not just another throw away slogan or something we learn in seminars and workshops. How we think is more than metaphysical. Our thinking creates a blueprint for taking action and gives us the ability to make things happen.

Mistakes Are Learning Experiences

The problem in our education system is it punishes for making mistakes. The grading system is mostly memory intensive, not creativity and innovation focused. Educators do not encourage risk taking and stress safety and compliance.

Thomas Edison made 1,000 mistakes before he discovered how to make a light bulb work. Making mistakes is a precursor to success. You cannot win if you do not try. People with persistence, desire, and commitment become winners because they *do* try.

The more mistakes you make, the faster you figure out what is the right thing to do. Mistakes are learning experiences. Keep a positive perspective.

The batting average of .300 in baseball is considered good; an average over .400 is nearly an unachievable goal. The last player that did it was Ted Williams of the Boston Red Sox in 1941 who hit a .406. The average batter is not hitting 70% of the time! Anyone who thinks they come close to 100% perfection of their actions is kidding themselves. Mistakes are a part of taking risks. Learning from them is how we gain knowledge.

When you look at mistakes as a normal course of events, you see it is not the end to anything. An important word to use in overcoming adversity and making mistakes is simply, "Next!"

Life Is Like a Bowl of Cherries

However with cherries, you also get the cherry pits. Life is a series of doors you open and like any game, sometimes you win, sometimes you lose.

Your thinking is what helps you through the adversity. Become self-reliant and remain optimistic or you will quit at the first sign of failure and tough times. Obstacles in your way are not a statement of fact you cannot get through them. Obstacles are only something that is in the way.

No Free Lunch

Expect good things to happen but be prepared for the worst. You can have almost anything you want as long as you are willing to go for it. However, it's not how hard you work that makes you a winner, it's how smart you work that gets you to your goals.

We get no free lunch. If you have rich parents and they made it easy for you, that may be wonderful, *until you are at a point you have to do things for yourself.* Having a past life of ease is one thing. Facing the reality of life's difficulties on your own are two very different things.

Overcoming everyday conflicts and stress of life is a learned skill. You may have to unlearn the easy way in order to get to the real way most people spend their lives accomplishing goals.

Life is going to give you disappointment, disruptions, and problems. Things will happen that you have no control over. It's how you react to what happens that makes you a winner. How you respond to difficulties and setbacks is as important to success as what is handed to you as a gift.

If you are not successful, you may feel like a victim and hurt but survivors get over this feeling. No one cares about your feeling sorry for yourself. Everyone has their own problems and dramas to deal with; they do not need yours.

Like going to the gym and working out, it will do you little good if you don't work out as hard as you can. You build yourself up and push yourself or you will not develop muscle. Overcoming adversity helps develop strength, just like bodybuilding and lifting weights develops muscles.

If you want to get ahead of average, it will take strength. The key is making commitments and not giving up when things get tough. Commitments go hand in hand with persistence.

Commitment Without Persistence Means Little

Your desire to be successful has to be strong. Desire is what motivates you and keeps you going. However, if you are not persistent, you need to develop that strength. Life will keep throwing you curve balls. Things will be in your face repeatedly.

Winners let adversity bounce off them and keep on going. Creating wealth and riches is going to take all the power and inner strength you can develop. Creating wealth is a marathon and a way of thinking.

Prepare yourself to stay in the race until you cross the finish line. Beware of negative environments and people who behave as the crabs stuck in a pot. Think positive and success, not failure.

Winners do not necessarily have a defined time frame; they keep running at the goal. Develop a strong desire and commitment. Above all, be persistent.

This is the lesson: never give in, never give in, never, never, never, never—in nothing, great or small, large or petty—never give in except to convictions of honour and good sense. Never yield to force; never yield to the apparently overwhelming might of the enemy.
—Winston Churchill

Rich and Free Entrepreneur's Guide

- Stay the course.
- Success is not about how long it takes.
- Most people daydream about getting Rich while few attempt it.
- Adversity makes people stronger.
- We get no free lunches.

Chapter 2

Good Communication Skills are Essential

I remind myself every morning: Nothing I say this day will teach me anything. So if I'm going to learn, I must do it by listening.

—**Larry King**

People with strong communication skills are most admired, make more money, and attract more opportunities. Effective speaking is expected, selling ideas and influencing others is essential.

Communicating is a learned skill, not born talent. You learn how to communicate from your environment. The workplace, friends, school, parents, and media influence your style. The successful in business, like professional athletes, work to improve their natural abilities. Becoming a better communicator takes drill and practice. Understanding why some people are better communicators than others will help improve your skills.

The paradox is, being a good communicator is not just about speaking and presenting. It is about being an active listener.

The better you interact with others, the more you learn from others.

Words Are Power

The spoken word is more powerful than the written word. Speaking it is an intellectual and behavioral process. We speak with the ability to evoke emotions of enthusiasm, sadness, anger, and excitement. When you hear the spoken voice and see power and emotion in people, you get real communication.

Luckily, you do not need a professional radio or TV announcer's voice. You do not need a good physical appearance to communicate and speak well. However, you need clear thoughts and well-formed sentences. Communicating is not about slickness, it is about how clearly you express ideas and thoughts. You need to be real and project passion. Simple and clear is what makes great speakers and good communicators.

Less Is More

The quality of information we communicate is how people judge us, not the quantity. Those who are able to *explain concepts in simple terms are the gifted communicators*. Be able to explain your visions clearly.

The Gettysburg address was only 286 words. Winston Churchill's "blood, sweat, and tears" speech to the British Parliament was 627 words and lasted only 6 minutes. You do not want people to think, "Why doesn't he just tell us what matters and get it over with?" Choose your words carefully, edit your thoughts and say what needs to be said.

Speaking is more powerful and effective when it is focused and concise. John F. Kennedy's, "My fellow Americans, ask not what your country can do for you; ask what you can do for your country," or Ronald Reagan telling Gorbachev to "Tear down this wall" were brilliant focused thoughts that had a point with very few words.

Hearing Is Not Listening

People talk at 150 to 180 words a minute yet hear and understand words spoken many times faster. They easily race ahead of thoughts in conversation and many are only listening to reply, not to understand. Many listen passively out of habit and are only interested in what *they* have to say. Passive listeners rarely acknowledge what others have said.

The successful make a major distinction between hearing and listening: much of our success comes from knowledge and information we get from others. Winners do not want to miss important communications and have learned how to be active listeners. Active listening requires concentration and focus and that is what enables you to comprehend more than spoken words.

What Is Active Listening?

Experts claim only 7% of communication is verbal, 35% is tone and emotion. The rest is body language. *The majority of communication is not spoken.* When someone is speaking with folded arms, laughing, grinning, starting to pace around, winking, growling, or raising their eyebrows, they are telling you more than they are saying. It's up to you to listen. Active listening is both listening to what is said and watching the emotions. Many subtleties are not the spoken word.

It's Never the Story, It's Always the Emotion

Communication may be more than the spoken word. Listen to what people *say* but look for the communication of how people *feel*. The intensity of emotions will tell you what people are really saying. A hypochondriac had his tombstone in Key West, Florida read:

> *I told you I was sick.*
> **—B. Pearl Roberts**

Listening actively enables a better environment for others to communicate with you. The more attention you give, the more others will return. People enjoy speaking to others that are interested in what they are saying. An active listener spends more time listening than talking.

Communication skills are a tool. It is how you sell ideas and influence people. Focus on improving communication ability. Some attend special classes while others may have private coaches. You cannot lead if you cannot influence others. Generating enthusiasm and a sense of urgency is critical.

Sell Your Image, Sell Your Ideas

A strong self-image is vital, the data and information you possess will not guarantee your success. It is your ability to *sell your ideas* that matters. If you want to be in high gear, you need to sell yourself, your ideas, and concepts.

Thinking bold is not speaking loudly or unprofessionally; *it's about style*. Good ideas combined with energy and emotions are what it takes to convince others to your way of thinking. Learn how to sell yourself with honesty and integrity and show excitement, energy and enthusiasm. The concept of selling is misunderstood and unfortunately, for many, it is exactly the skill needed to create wealth.

Communication Is Active Listening and Getting Ideas Across

It's not only what you say; it's how *others* perceive you. Good communication skills are an important element for development of relationships. Both the listener and speaker must work at developing good verbal and listening skills.

Communicating ideas brings our minds together but communicating emotions brings us together as individuals. Emotions are powerful and they cannot be ignored, don't put yourself first:

> **To Have Others Feel Good About You,
> Express Empathy and Show Interest In Them**

The following are keys to effective communications. These ideas will help you position your thoughts. When you become a better listener, it allows you to influence others. However, just reading these points will not improve your communication skills, practice them until they become habits.

Keys to Effective Communications

Use Your Body

Eye contact, facial expressions, body, and posture
are all part of communication. Speak with clarity
and try to say more with fewer words. Take a
breath, use pauses for emphasis. Give people a
chance to respond to what you say and do not
babble on and overrun your good ideas and
thoughts. You should never use a continuous
monotone voice; vary your loudness, pitch, and
tone. Exude energy, enthusiasm, and confidence
when appropriate. Your body dominates you; it is
your overwhelming feature. Use your personal
impact to make your points.

Find Common Ground

Active listeners plan a response after others finish
speaking. Avoid the trap of interrupting, be sure of
what others have said. Listen and understand
people so you can position the conversation to a
middle or common ground. This common ground
enables you to talk from the same viewpoint or
perspective of others. It shows you understand
what is said. It makes communication easier to
continue from both sides. Pace the speaking tone to
be compatible with others or they may tune you
out.

Acknowledge What Others Say

When you acknowledge others, you are enhancing
your own position. Nothing is more important to
others than hearing their own names and being

understood. When people speak, acknowledge what they are saying, show interest, and respond. This is much more powerful than people realize. Being receptive to other points of view is paramount. Ask questions, stay alert, and suspend judgment. Do not jump to conclusions before you are sure you understand what others are saying.

Respect Different Viewpoints

Do not listen just to get information to support your ideas or points of view. It shows disrespect, and stops you from seeing things from a different perspective. Everyone is entitled to his or her point of view, right or wrong. Listening actively only means you are trying to understand. Paying attention demonstrates you are respectful enough to hear others' ideas and opinions but it does not mean you have to agree with them. Business relationships are built on common ground and diversity. Different ideas and opinions create synergy, the foundation of all business. Do not try to make others conform to all of your ideas and you will earn new friends and respect.

Stay on Topic

Good communicators do not change the subject of conversation in mid-stream; they wait for the other person to complete the thought or idea. If you change the subject before others are finished, you are saying, "I don't care what you just said" or "I have something more important to say than you do." Change the subject before it's time and you will likely lose the rest of the conversation or communication.

Don't Trump Others

"I can top that" puts you in a poor position. When someone tells you they just got back from London, you can say, "Where did you stay, what did you do?" Or you can say, "We went from London to Santorini in the Greek Islands," to top what was just said. Do not try and top the conversation or people will be wishing they were anywhere other than talking to you. To be interesting, be interested and add to the conversation. Acknowledge what is said.

Raise the Gradient Slowly

Remember the story of the frog and the boiling water. If you put a frog in a pot of hot boiling water, it will jump out. However, if you put a frog in a pot of cool water and slowly turn up the heat, the frog will slowly get accustomed to the temperature rising. The frog never feels the heat rising. That heat rising is the gradient. Slowly raise intensity and ideas when you meet people, or they will jump out of the pot. Until you understand where others are coming from, raise the gradient slowly or you can wind up shooting yourself in the foot and scaring people away.

Never Talk in Absolutes

Talking in absolutes is a subtle turn off and you can easily avoid this mistake. However, many are oblivious they are even doing it. When you speak, use open terms. Let others have their own opinion and thoughts. Speaking in absolute terms ends the communication as you have spoken for others. You never know what others are thinking; you can only assume what they are thinking. Speak in terms of, "I have an idea, let's... or "We should look at this problem and see if we can..." Do not start thoughts with definitive answers, "I know we all feel this way." That is not a good opener for conversation and shows you are insensitive to others. It's easy to change the tone and positioning. "Some of us feel this way," works every time and makes your point.

Look to Resolve Differences

Be conscious of compromising people when you speak, it creates a win-lose situation. Make it a habit to create alternatives or new viewpoints when you have disagreements. Belligerence is a bad tactic to resolve things. If you win a point or discussion, leave something on the table so you can build relationships. When you compromise people, especially in front of others, you may win the battle, but you will lose the war. Find points you can mutually agree on.

Watch Your Temper

Your good qualities are preempted when tempers are hot as you are communicating to everyone, "I'm out of control," and "You can't trust me." With a bad temper, people under you will be afraid of you. Superiors will be nervous to have you in a position of authority. Bad tempers are not good for business and a quick tongue and temper can be the "Kiss of Death" for a career.

Keep Your Ego in Check

Everyone needs a strong ego; it is the critical edge for speakers and communicators. You cannot think of yourself as insignificant if you want to become a mountain of strength. However, if this great strength is overused, it can become an Achilles heel. When egos are out of control, it is difficult to get honest communication as you have put others on defense. Show humility, affinity, and compassion. The more authority you have, the more carefully you have to watch your speech and behavior. Big egos out of control are shown the door as soon as others can open it.

Electronic and Digital Communication

With new technologies, many use blogging, text messaging, pagers and email. The computer keyboard is an important way to say things and communicate. More and more people are doing "stuff" not face to face. Many successful people use the computer as a medium but they have already mastered the skills of verbal communication. But others with less experience may not have the communication skills and body language important for good speaking. The electronic media has made it easy to let personal skills lapse or not be developed. People say things behind a keyboard they will never say in person. Your ideas will not mean a lot if you cannot hold a good conversation. Be sure you do not replace electronic communication for real world speaking. Learn to do both well.

Build a Strong Foundation

You do not have to be a professional presenter, however to be an effective speaker you need to be a very good listener. The ability to communicate well is the ability to sell your ideas, talk to customers and financial people. Selling ideas and yourself is what creates success. When dealing with professionals, be a professional.

Rich and Free
Entrepreneur's Guide

- Good communicators have the ability to sell themselves and influence others.
- The secret to communication: become an active listener.
- Pay attention to *everything* when people speak.
- Details are often spoken in emotions.
- Clarity is power: speak less - say more.

Chapter 3

The Art of Negotiating

The one sure way to conciliate a tiger is to allow oneself to be devoured.

—Konrad Adenauer (1876-1967)

John Godfrey Saxe, 1816-1887, made a famous Chinese parable into a poem. The story from the Han Dynasty 202 BC:

The Blind Men and the Elephant

A long time ago in India, six blind men lived in a village. One day, the blind men heard an elephant had wandered into town. These blind men had no idea what an elephant was, so they decided to go for a visit. Even though they could not see the elephant, they would be able to feel it and discover what it was.

The first blind man felt the tail and said, "I found a rope!"

The second said, "It's a tree!" as he touched the elephant's knee.

"It's a big fan!" said the third blind man as he touched one of the elephant's ears.

The fourth man found a squirming trunk and said, "It must be a snake!"

The fifth touched the sharp tusk and said, "It's very much like a spear!"

And the sixth blind man said, "No, no, you're all wrong, it must be a wall!" as he ran his hands over the elephant's body.

The men continued to argue over what the elephant was. A wise man walking by overheard the discussion.

"What is the matter?" the wise man asked.

"We all see the elephant differently, and we can't agree on what it is," the blind men replied.

The wise man thought about the problem and said, "As each of you has touched a different part of the elephant, each of you has a different understanding of what it is. You are all right, and you are all wrong. The elephant is larger and more complex than any one of you realize."

What You See Depends

Each of us creates our own versions of reality. We see things through our paradigms and filters of experience and interests. We are blind to the totality of what we deal with. We often make conclusions from images that are subjective at best. It's human nature to make judgments, even on partial information.

Negotiating is like the blind men understanding the elephant. Everyone negotiates but few gain enough insight to understand all of it. For most people, negotiating is difficult. It's like speaking in public; the thought of it turns stomachs and creates anxiety.

Why Negotiating Skills Are Important

If you were to ask an entrepreneur or business owner, what is the one critical skill to have, the answer may surprise you. It's negotiating!

In business, you negotiate. Anything can be negotiated. The more successful you get, the more negotiation you will do. Success brings power. With power, you are in a position to negotiate. The more power you have, the more you need negotiating skills.

Negotiating is a way to get things done without a legal fight. It's a way to come to an understanding about problems and opportunities.

Negotiating is Not Litigating

Litigating is a formal legal process. It deals with lawsuits, claims, and arguments that usually end with a winner and a loser.

Negotiating is a process to create co-operation and agreement. It takes many forms. We use negotiations to set schedules and priorities, create contracts, settle differences, establish prices, set standards, buy things and sell things. Anything can be negotiated.

Don't Be Afraid To Negotiate

In successful negotiations, everyone wins something but no one has victory over the other. The goal is to manage conflict, hostilities, and disagreements. Successful negotiations create a better environment to get along with bosses, people at work, friends, and family.

No one is born with negotiating skills but with practice and experience, you can greatly improve them. Negotiating impacts every aspect of your life, it's how you express your desires, wants, and needs. People rely on negotiating skills to influence others, and make business deals work.

Business is Not Fair or Democratic

With experience, almost everyone comes to the same conclusion: business is not fair or democratic, it's a competitive game of opportunity.

> **You Get What You Negotiate,
> Not What You Deserve.**

The frog explains why negotiating is more than a skill, it's a process:

A Frog Tale

**Two frogs fell into a deep cream bowl,
One was an optimistic soul,
But the other took a gloomy view,
We shall drown he cried, without more adieu!**

**So with a last despairing cry,
He flung up his legs and said "goodbye"**

Said the frog with a merry grin,
I can't get out, but I won't give in,
I'll just swim around till my strength is spent,
Then I will die the more content.

Bravely he swam till it did seem,
His struggling began to churn the cream,
On top of the butter at last he stepped,
And out of the bowl at last he leapt.

What of the moral? 'Tis easily found,
If you can't get out... keep swimming around!

Setting Up Your Platform

Negotiating is art, not science, be *prepared to be surprised.* Emotions and egos are a perfect setup for spontaneously unpredictable things to happen. You are looking to get yourself into the best position to win or take a pass. Do not get lost in what was "supposed" to be.

Negotiating has no "Rules of the game," they are non-existent and are made up as you go along. Make a list of ideas and positions that support what you want to accomplish so you will not be distracted. More often than not, the winner will be the one with the best skills, not the best position.

Think of a negotiation as a game of football. You see the goal line but you are going to have a hard time trying to make a beeline for it. It might take yard after yard of grinding effort to make progress or it can happen on one big play. Success may well depend on how prepared you are and how you think on your feet.

A classic position of negotiators is to have an attitude, *it's only a game.* A game has less importance than real life since you can stop playing any time and walk away. It can be intimidating to face an attitude like this, but don't let it make you defensive; it's a ploy. People are only at the negotiating table because they think they have something to gain or win. Arrogance and aggressive behavior in negotiations is a weak position and good negotiators will see right through it. Hot air does not solve problems. Don't be too powerful for your own good and never underestimate your opposition.

Think Like Colombo, Not Dress Like Him

Colombo from the TV series won cases. He appeared to be a scatter-brained, frumpy, cigar smoking, disheveled hayseed. However, his appearance was deceiving and hid a brilliant cat-and-mouse player. The other side underestimated his prowess and abilities as he went after details and mechanics of the mind. He never showed off. The calm methodical bulldog approach of finding answers was the key to his success and much like the skills of a good negotiator. Unlike the capable high tech forensic TV detectives of today, Colombo was a personal train wreck. You could not stop watching his apparent ineptitude.

Tipping your hat to how capable you are might get others working harder to beat you. Keep your ego under control. Save your knowledge and preparation for the right time.

You Can't Argue with a Blank Wall

Look beyond negotiating positions or standpoints. When you discover the interest of others, you may find compromise and resolve issues. Getting someone off a position is very hard unless you know why he or she has that position. In negotiations, many people do not ask an important question:

Why Are Others Asking For What They Want?

When you discover *why* people are asking for what they want, you may be able to find resolutions that will work for both sides. A position or demand can be a blank wall. You cannot argue with it. Find out what is *behind* the wall. Listen intently until you discover why the other party is at the table.

Insight will make the difference and people skills will most likely be your strongest asset in negotiating. Everyone has different personality styles and traits. Determine how your behavior affects others and adjust your style and behavior accordingly. Communication success is how well you relate and interface with others.

It's simple to understand others' behavior and personality styles as long as you don't try to over think and play psychoanalyst. People are far too complex to figure out.

When trying to understand others, keep it simple. It's like painting the walls in a house with a wide paint roller instead of using a fine artist's paintbrush. You're trying to get an overview of people you're dealing with.

People may change their dominant style or use a combination of styles to accommodate a situation, be patient. In time, people's personalities tend to show through, especially under stress. Have this thought in mind when you talk to people: what kind of communicators are they and what kind of personalities or styles do they have? Look for style and adjust to it, but don't over think it and don't make it obvious. Almost everyone will fit into one of four dominant styles:

Common Behavior and Personality Styles:

- **The Controlling Style**, aggressive, dominant, get it done now, "it's my way or the highway"

- **The Reserved Style**, steady, methodical, team player

- **The Talkative Style**, influencing, tries to motivate others, wants you to like them

- **The Introverted Style**, cautious, conscientious, detail oriented, "show me how" attitude

You can't change what you are and people may see through you if you try. However, you can subtly *adjust* your style and that is all it takes to be effective. You are trying to get the piano in tune so it will play better. You do not want personality styles and friction blocking the negotiating process.

Adjusting to Different Styles:

- **Aggressive Personalities:** they want fast answers and no flowers. Get to the point quickly, no chit chats.

- **Talkative and People Oriented:** be friendly and social but do not underestimate them, they may be trying to sell you to their positions.

- **Good Listeners:** be calm and steady as they are reserved. Slow down and control enthusiasm.

- **Introverted and Sticklers for Detail:** be factual and specific. Everything you say may be challenged. Choose your words and details carefully.

Be an Active Listener

You learn real interests of others when you are an active and intent listener. Tone of voice and body language are the real keys to understanding communication. Be alert, listen intently, and watch closely.

> **Never Interrupt Others When They are Making Mistakes**

When you're the active listener, others are doing the talking. They can talk themselves into a corner. Talk less and listen more, you will be less likely to make mistakes. Let the other party make the mistakes for you.

Key Negotiating Points:

- **Know what you want.** What will be the best outcome ? Know why this is important to you.

- **Find out what the other side wants as soon as possible.** The other side would not be there if they had nothing to gain. What are they after?

- **Your power is your walk-away alternative.** You never disclose this. If the deal or the situation is not possible, what is your next best choice? At what point will you walk away.

- **Do not allow authority or status to intimidate you.** Your point of view or issues are not less important because you are dealing with powerful people.

- **If you are in a powerful position, do not let it go to your head.** Remember how Colombo won. Keep your ego in check.

- **Be suspicious of deadlines.** They may be phony and a ploy to pressure others into making bad decisions if time runs out. Challenge unfavorable timetables.

- **Listen intently.** This is your most important skill. If you know you have a problem listening (and you know who you are) practice before negotiating. Make *active listening* your biggest asset.

- **People are poor listeners.** Be sure you are getting your ideas across.

- **Be reasonable and flexible.** Look for a satisfying agreement for both parties.

- **Negotiation is a process not an event.** Remember the frog in the bowl of cream. Exhaust every opportunity to win or resolve the issues.

- **Deal honestly and ethically.** Deal with integrity; you may need future opportunities to negotiate.

- **Leave something on the table.** If you are ever planning to do business with someone again, remember negotiating is not poker where winner takes all.

- **Put it in writing.** Write a note of understanding immediately what has been agreed upon.

Negotiations are subjective and a process. Keep it simple, focused, and use common sense. Your people skills and the ability to read others may be your strongest assets.

The skills of negotiating become more important as you achieve success and create wealth. Like any skill, it takes practice and drill to become a professional. Negotiating is a skill you master for *your own protection as well as your success.*

Negotiating is a skill that helps jobs and careers but it is a must-have *essential skill* as an entrepreneur. The rich and successful work at mastering negotiating skills and it will help you become more successful as well.

Rich and Free
Entrepreneur's Guide

- You get what you negotiate, not what you deserve.
- Lawyers litigate, everyone else negotiates.
- Strong people skills are the secret to winning negotiations.
- Experienced negotiators are the active listeners, not fastest talkers.
- The rich and successful master negotiating skills.

Chapter 4

Brainstorming and Masterminding: The Mind Game to Creating Wealth

Talent wins games, but teamwork and intelligence wins championships.
                                          —Michael Jordan

While managing a radio station in Washington, DC, I hired a programming consultant. His name was E. Karl and he was an expert in strategic planning and research. When I became President of Viacom Radio in New York, I asked E. to help us with all of our stations. We were spending hundreds of thousand of dollars on research. I wanted professional expertise and experience to help us make sense of the mountains of data we were getting from our research.

Research does not end when focus groups or strategic studies finish. It is just starting. The key to successful research is in the interpreting. Collecting data is easy; understanding it is the hard part.

Our research projects had a team of people. While we all looked at the same information, many times we came to different conclusions about what the data meant. As everyone was seeing things through their own perspective, we often used a consensus to make decisions.

Why Airline Lasagna Tastes That Way

There may be danger with group thinking; it depends on your goals. Consensus leans towards safety; group thinking may distract you from taking calculated risks. A team might not be able to make good entrepreneurial calls as it may lead to mediocre or safe conclusions. I mentioned my concerns to E. about risk taking and playing it safe. He told me a story.

"Do you know how they make airline lasagna?" E. asked.

"No," I said.

E. said, "It works like this."

"When you have a lot of money at stake and a lot is riding on decisions, get a bunch of expert opinions. The thinking is, the more opinions, the better. Therefore, the airlines serving lasagna lunches and dinners by the tens of thousands, made sure the people responsible for creating the airline food called in the best chefs to get the best ideas. The goal: make a dish that will taste good to everyone."

"The airlines use the best of the ideas and came up with great tasting lasagna for everyone. Actually, when you put all the thinking together, you wind up with a lot of compromising. What you come up with is an *average tasting lasagna that won't offend anyone*," E. said.

"Airline food is safe food. Not a lot of spices to get anyone upset. It tastes OK, but hardly award winning. If you want great tasting lasagna, you need spices and that means taking some risks. When you spice things up, some people will love the dish even more and some will not like it at all. It is a risk you take. Successful ideas can never please everyone. If you try to please all, you become average."

Risk More Often, Win More Often

What E. was saying is when you have too many chefs in the kitchen, group decisions will more often than not come to a safe conclusion. I have seen this phenomenon happen repeatedly. Groupthink may distract you from leading edge thinking; it tends to be conservative and safe while setting high goals usually means taking more risks.

Monkey Business

My experience is successful people share the wealth and resources. If you hold on to your money and ideas too tight, you wind up like the monkeys in the Amazon.

A story of greed is how natives catch small monkeys in the jungle. Monkeys are hard to catch. They swing high in the trees and avoid danger. Natives take a coconut, drill a hole in it the size of a quarter, and put two peanuts inside.

They hang the coconut from a tree branch. The monkeys will be curious and when no one is around, they shake the coconut and hear the peanuts inside. Once they put their little hand inside and grab the peanut, their hand become so big they cannot get it out of the hole.

The natives come back and find the monkeys hanging from the coconuts. They simply cut the string, as the monkey will not let go of the peanuts. The monkey cannot escape.

Don't Play for Peanuts

People not willing to share ideas will often hang on to peanut ideas. Success escapes them; they are caught holding on to nothing. They have nowhere to go for help.

However, when good ideas work, you will not be able to spend the money fast enough much less worry about having to share success with others. Do not let greed and control stop you from masterminding with others.

Masterminding Is About Quality Thinking

An important point in masterminding is you only need a small group or just one other person to help you, not a big team. Masterminding and brainstorming is not a contact sport. You do not need lots of body mass. It's a mind game and only takes a few good thinkers.

Masterminding is the leverage of minds. The collective thinking creates synergy. The aggressive "I can do it myself" personalities usually do wind up doing it by themselves, but with limited success.

Behind the "Lone Ranger" thinking may be a different motive. Greed. People may not want to share ideas, wealth, or riches.

Masterminding became famous when Napoleon Hill wrote *Think and Grow Rich* in 1937. Napoleon inspired by the great industrialist Andrew Carnegie, studied rich and wealthy people over a twenty-year period. Meeting with so many successful people gave Napoleon insight how all the outrageously wealthy had made their riches. He discovered they all had something in common. The rich surrounded themselves with a small group of creative and innovative like-minded people for ideas, support, experience, and suggestions. The rich were all brainstorming and masterminding ideas and theories.

Creating wealth is a mind game. Learning how to think better is like learning how to play tennis. If you want to improve your tennis game, play with people who play better than you. Challenge yourself. The more you challenge yourself, the better you become.

Bill Gates of Microsoft, Michael Dell of Dell computer, President Theodore Roosevelt, John D. Rockefeller, and Winston Churchill all used the power of masterminding, brainstorming, and collective thinking.

> **Your Greatest Assets Are The People Around You And The People You Are Around.**

So if this concept works so well, why don't they teach it in schools? They should! In school, they call it cheating if you took a test with people you trusted to help you. In business, we call it strategic thinking and planning. We get people together to work out ideas and strategies. It matters little where ideas and strategies come from; it is only what you do with the ideas and will they work that matters.

It will be difficult to get to the top of the game without the help of smart creative people. This concept is critically important in times of change where simple ideas teamed with good business practices can make millions in a very short period. With better tools, computers, software, and a worldwide market, it's no wonder well managed ideas create wealth so much faster than past generations.

What may stop you from taking the first step is you may be bashful, timid or you may not trust your instincts. However, when you challenge yourself, others may be more willing to help you.

Like-minded does not mean *same* minded. There is always a different way to see things. It's important to share ideas with others with different opinions even at the risk of being shot down. People looking to achieve wealth and riches often face frustration and overwhelm. It takes a strong will to do what others fear or cannot conceive.

Everyone Needs Encouragement

Most people are on the path of average. If you do something different, do not think others will help you until they see things working. That is why having a small group of like-minded thinkers to meet with will help you get started and keep you going.

It is important to have encouragement. Working with others will give you positive thoughts and energy. And of course, working alone is lonely!

I worked for Woody Sudbrink and Hal Gore of Sudbrink Broadcasting. They were my mentors, and bosses. Woody was the owner, Hal was the President. I was very young when I started with them, I did not understand the concept of masterminding.

In time, I began to understand the differences in Woody and Hal's personalities and styles. They focused on the same goals but they were night and day different people. With Woody, you could always smell the wood burning. His mind was laser focused on business. It was not that he had poor people skills; it was his vision to focus on elements of the business.

Hal was the ultimate people person. His skills were more than business experience. His leadership and people skills made things happen in the company.

Hal did most of the interfacing with the managers; Woody did the work in the background. They masterminded the business strategy, but managed the business through personalities. Hal and Woody complimented each other and were able go about making the business successful through each of their unique strengths.

If you feel your strength is not in managing others, you will only hurt your efforts if you try to manage because your ego says you can do anything. Some of us are better at some things than others. It's important to understand others but it is critical to understand your own strengths and limitations.

Masterminding is not to find people like yourself that agree with everything you believe in. Find people with the same goals and if possible, people who are smarter than you are. Their talent and brains are your gain, not your competition.

Woody and Hal made an extraordinary team and masterminded everything in the business yet managed to be independent people. The business grew better through their collective efforts of masterminding.

I saw a similar masterminding relationship when I managed KOOL radio in Phoenix, Arizona with Bob Hughes and Jonathon Schwartz, owners of Compass Radio.

Bob is a programmer, literate and a very right brain. Jonathan is an investment banker and left-brain analytical thinker. As different as they are, they complimented each other and the two of them together created synergy. Each of them needed the other's skills; together they were stronger than working alone.

What worked for them was the ability to mastermind the problems from two entirely different perspectives. At times, each of them took the other's role.

Either one of them could easily have run the company, but both of them ran it better and accomplished higher goals and success. In the end, the collective thinking was brilliant and made a little company a big success. Their collective strengths helped them deal with the adversity of bankers and capitalist that may have been able to run over and overwhelm one person. As a team, Bob and Jonathan were stronger than any one person; they masterminded their way to success.

People are Leverage

No one is an island but plenty of people think they are. All you have to do is look at the limitations and problems people create for themselves with this thinking. No one has all the skills to do it alone. You can remain independent and work with others; you still make your own decisions.

Working with others extends ideas and improves perspective. With the expertise and experience of others, ideas become leveraged. One person cannot conceive of every angle or concept in business or investing. *It takes more than one person to create synergy and leverage.*

Corporate Survival Strategy May Have To Be Unlearned

If you have spent years in a competitive cutthroat company, masterminding is a concept you may have been avoiding. Sharing information with others that are directly competitive to your job or career may cause you problems. In some careers and political environments, it may even be dangerous to share ideas.

Your ideas may bring information that others will steal, or even used against you. Working in corporate environments may call for different strategies. One of them is not allowing others to take your ideas and jump over you. This is a real problem and happens all too often.

Politics in the office place is a handicap for the company. Individuals, for survival, put themselves ahead of company success to protect jobs and careers. The rules of winning in a corporate environment are often political and not entrepreneurial.

Behind the Scenes

Behind every winner, it's a good bet someone is in the background helping. The successful have experience and know the secret is from the inside looking out:

We Are All Alone. Together.

We have all heard the idiom, "Great minds think alike," but more often than not, my experience has been that great minds often do not always think alike. I have seen great minds with common goals but great thinkers are unique. Often they will not follow rules and consensus.

It takes time to understand and let go of old thinking. Experience proves that people are more important than ideas. Ideas bring people together.

The secret of the rich and successful is they do not try to do it alone:

King Arthur and the Round Table

Our Founding Fathers and *The Decoration of Independence*

Jason and Argonauts

Board of Directors

Board of Advisors

Key Reasons to Mastermind

1. **Creating wealth comes from knowledge, information, and wisdom directed with sound business principles.**

2. **Diverse opinions may bring critical input.**

3. **Two or more people can create infinite intelligence and wisdom that few accomplish on their own.**

4. **Experience accumulates with masterminding.**

5. **Everyone adds value, you don't learn less.**

6. **Masterminding environments allows bigger goals.**

7. **Self-made millionaires do not exist in real life, it's team-made millionaires.**

8. **Working with others is the ultimate form of leverage.**

9. **Masterminding creates power. Power is essential to creating wealth.**

Are You Afraid of Power?

The rich and wealthy have power. It takes power to make things happen and translate plans and ideas into action.

Many fear power based on other people's envy. Others fear it because they have never had it. Believing you can be powerful is emotional and can be intimidating. These emotions and fears are real enough but hardly a reason to stop you. Power is what you make it.

Fear of power will stop you from greater accomplishments. If you fear directing your ideas into power, you may never achieve success. You need power not only to create wealth, but also to keep wealth.

Masterminding will help you accomplish goals that may be impossible to achieve on your own. When you have money and wealth, you become the 800-pound gorilla. You can do what you like and sit anywhere you want. Power does not have to be abusive but if you want to get rich, it's going to take one heck of a lot of power to get there. Masterminding is a very powerful concept used by the very rich and successful. Use it to create your freedom and independence, share the wealth, and get even richer.

Rich and Free Entrepreneur's Guide

- Large group thinking tends to be safe and consensus.
- Masterminding is a very small group of focused people.
- Find bright people with diverse opinions and experience that share your goals.
- Masterminding is leverage and synergy.
- Power is essential to creating wealth.

Chapter 5

The Power of Specialized Knowledge

Information is a source of learning. But unless it is organized, processed, and available to the right people in a format for decision making, it is a burden, not a benefit.

—William Pollard

Learn to "Run the Numbers." They will tell you where you have been, where you are, and help project the future. Numbers are critical to running a business, managing money, and evaluating investments. Numbers become specialized knowledge when you learn how to use them as a tool. They help you spot problems and uncover opportunities.

I discovered that my ability to deal with numbers improved when I saw the data and information as pictures. I put numbers into charts and graphs. As a dyslexic, my ability to make sense of data or raw numbers was confusing; I was not able to make meaningful distinctions. Once I was able to convert numbers to pictures, my disadvantage became an advantage; I was able to turn information into knowledge.

Two Numbers Do Not make a Trend

When you draw a line between two numbers, you see point A connected to point B. When you add a third number, you may find some useful information. Three connected lines may tell you things are wildly unpredictable or they may show the beginning of a trend. When you deal with lots of numbers, it may be overwhelming.

Managing broadcast companies, we lived and died with ratings. Rating and research gave us massive amounts of information. Often the critical information hid in the data. In order to make better decisions, I became an expert in computer graphics and spreadsheets. Turning data into pictures gives numbers dimension. We were able to make informed strategic decisions because we were able to convert information into something useful.

The Problem is Not Information, it's Overload.

Information is readily available but without the ability to filter data, it is just information. Data by itself is a meaningless point in time and space that has no reference or context without the understanding of relationships. In business and investing, learn how to project what you think will happen over time.

Predictable patterns give the potential to gain knowledge. This concept is especially true in research where gathering information is simple and readily available. The key is how to relate and interpret information and turn it into usable knowledge. The skill in research is in the interpretation, not in gathering data or information.

Computers Have Little Reasoning and Even Less Judgment

Regardless how powerful a computer is or the mountains of information and data you gather, it will never take the place of reasoning, judgment, and perceptions. Information is only as good as you can evaluate, interpret, and understand. Wisdom comes from learning and the experience of doing things.

During the 1980's and early 1990's, IBM had as much information as any computer company in business. They let Microsoft become the software giant by focusing on machine sales and overlooking the value of software and intellectual property. It was a huge mistake and oversight. IBM had information but did not have the knowledge or wisdom to know what to do with it. They missed a multi-billion dollar operating software business. They were blinded by their own success.

IBM was focused on big computers. Their mainframe computers at the time were very profitable. They had the information that network computing was rising. PCs were growing in popularity, and getting more powerful. However, IBM refused to let go of an old way of doing business. It took years of new leadership to get them back on track.

With knowledge, you are able to gain wisdom. Wisdom is experience, insight, principles and morality. Wisdom comes from knowledge *and* experience.

Genius is making the difficult easy to see, not making the difficult even harder to comprehend.

> **Thinking Is Hard To Do.
> That Is Why We Are So Willing
> To Let Others Do It For Us.**

Creating wealth and independence is about your ability to think. You need financial skills to manage a business or put a venture together. Most businesses fail not because of information but lack of experience and knowledge on how to make things work. People win by learning more; they do not assume they know everything.

Business is not static. What works today may not be working tomorrow. The successful continually put the lines together on charts to see where things are going.

People get into trouble with *what they think they know.* They think they know enough about sales, marketing, finance, and operations but all they have is information with little knowledge. They are so sure they are right they spend time defending what they know to be the truth. When they make a mistake or fail, they justify their information but do not seek the education and knowledge to help them.

Knowledge is NOT Power!

Many misunderstand the saying of "Knowledge is Power." Knowledge is priceless as long as you realize it is only potential. It is what you do with your knowledge that matters. What you know does not count if you do not do anything with it.

You acquire information, organize it, and turn that information into making something happen. However, many have knowledge but are not motivated and lack drive, their powerful knowledge is useless. You do not have to know everything, just how to get the specialized knowledge you need to make you a success.

> **Ideas Are Important**
> **But Not As Important**
> **As Making Things Happen**

The knowledge how to make a business work is different from an idea. If you can cut a lawn, landscape a yard, or manage a garden, it means you know something about plants, gardening, and lawn cutting. It does not mean you know how to run a landscaping business.

You need specialized knowledge of plants, design and you need to know how to organize, run, and manage a landscape business to make a profit. Knowing a trade and turning a trade into a successful business are two entirely different skills. Each skill needs entirely different knowledge and experience to create success.

Not one engineer in the space shuttle effort ever became an astronaut; engineers and astronauts have different skills and knowledge. No modern day Indy 500 engineer or mechanic has become an Indy 500 race car driver.

Learn Specific Skills

You make the decisions on what you want to do. Do not be a procrastinator! Focus on the trade and skills that will make you rich. If you do not have those skills, go get them.

You may think you can be successful because you are a "Jack of All Trades" but most likely you will not be able to master even one of them. Acquire specialized knowledge and become good at a specific trade.

> **Become An Expert At One Thing But Build Collateral Skills As Well.**

Many today talk about the need to be knowledgeable in all areas of business as times are moving so fast. The argument is that learning the wrong skills may make you competent in the wrong area. That is fool's thinking. If you have mastered skills that become obsolete, *learn new skills that are not obsolete.*

However, not making a decision to become an expert in a specific field because of changing times is simply refusing to make a decision. You need knowledge about what you want to do. If you do not know enough, go and learn more.

We are living longer today. Things are changing more quickly than any time in history. You may find yourself in several careers in a lifetime. Learn how to be the best you can be at something that will create your wealth and give you freedom.

Business Has Attrition

A business does not stand still. Either it grows or it will go sideways and eventually sink. It is the law of attrition. You're not in business or a venture by yourself, you deal with competition.

A business is like an athlete. They not only play the sport, they train until they cannot keep up the strength and cannot play anymore. At a point when they cannot compete, they hand it over to younger players. In business, hand over responsibility to grow, or you will find yourself out of business.

Take generalized education and knowledge and get it laser focused on what you want to do. Learn the special skills of the business or venture you want to accomplish. Learn how to organize and run that specific business.

Many have ideas but let making money stop them. They will not work for knowledge or education. However, if you need a mentor or experience, you may want to consider what a doctor does.

Work for Free!

Doctors go to school for years to learn a trade. Doctors who specialize earn far more than general practitioners do. It is not a secret that brain surgeons make more than dentists do. However, it also takes a more specialized education to be a brain surgeon.

Interns learn from experienced doctors. What a doctor learns in college and medical school is specialized knowledge. Before an intern can become a doctor, they need real life experience. Interns are paid very little if anything. It is the knowledge and experience they gain interning that sets up their lifetime career.

If you want to learn how to do something, but lack the knowledge, think about doing what doctors do. Work for free or intern to gain the knowledge and experience you need. When you have specialized knowledge, it is your entry to creating wealth.

Being smart and having a formal education gets you a job. However, owning your own business or starting a venture has little to do with formal education. It has everything to do with specialized skills and the knowledge you gain from experience.

The more you know, the more others will invest in you and the more you will be willing to invest in yourself.

Rich and Free Entrepreneur's Guide

- Turn numbers into pictures so you can understand them better.
- Information is not knowledge.
- Knowledge is not power if you do nothing with it.
- Specialized knowledge is more than gathering information.
- Business has attrition, keep your education current.
- Work for free to get the knowledge and experience that may make you rich.

Chapter 6

Getting Ideas Organized

He has half the deed done who has made a beginning.
—Quintus Horatius Flaccus 65BC

Planning puts visions in order. It's the blueprint for taking action. However, before you start, you need to answer some questions. What do you want to do? What skills do you have? What do you need to learn? Do you have money to get started? Are you a self-starter? Can you lead others? Do you like to make decisions? Do you have the drive to keep yourself going? Are you good at organizing ideas?

A stalled career or one that never got off the ground may have you thinking, it's time to try something new. Not having been able to create wealth or independence may have you ready to go after what you want. If you are willing to change your thinking, you may be able to change your life.

That is Garbage!

Wayne Huizenga is the only person in history to have built three Fortune 1,000 companies from scratch. He started in 1962 with a single garbage truck! That started a trash-hauling multinational operation from Argentina to New Zealand. Wayne went on to build Blockbuster into a nationwide movie rental outlet and sold it to Viacom for $8.4 billion. His third act was starting AutoNation which put Ford, Chevy, and others together and created a new concept generating $20 billion in sales.

Wayne went from hauling garbage to renting videos to selling cars. Being an entrepreneur is limited by opportunity, there is no rulebook of ideas. You find them or you think them up.

> *Business opportunities are like buses, there's always another one coming.*
> —**Richard Branson**
> Virgin Group, English Entrepreneur

Opportunities multiply once you take action. The more you do, the more opportunities come to you. Things happen when you move forward; things that were invisible begin to appear.

Think Simple

It's human nature to make things complicated. It's the job of the entrepreneur to make them uncomplicated. Think simple:

> ## Your Job Is Not To Judge Others, It's To Profit From Them.
>
> 1. Find out what people want.
> 2. Go and get it.
> 3. Give it to them.

The idea is only one part of what will make a successful business. It's not difficult to barbeque a hamburger better than McDonalds. What makes McDonalds an extraordinary business *is the system*.

All businesses are a system. Every day a business opens for business, it does not reinvent the business. A system creates success. You do repeatedly what works. You do the same things until you find a better way to do them.

Some ideas are overlooked because they are boring or simple. However, that may be poor strategy. A boring, safe, profitable business can give you time and money to do other things. Need excitement? Consider skydiving on weekends. You want your ideas to make cash flow and earn a profit.

How to Plan Like an Entrepreneur

The plan has six parts, one page or less for each thought. Refine your thoughts, keep it precise and to the point. A CEO can get a billion dollar business concept on a 5x8 card; you can get your ideas on a few sheets of paper

This plan is designed to help you think if your idea has important elements to be a winner. It's not a formal business plan; it's a starting point to test ideas.

Testing Ideas

1. **What is the Exit Strategy?**
2. **Do I Have A Niche?**
3. **Am I Using Leverage?**
4. **Who Is On My Team?**
5. **How Do I Reach and Sell Customers?**
6. **Does My Idea Pass The Acid Test?**

Step #1. What is the Exit Strategy?

Begin your plan with an exit strategy and start with the end in mind. You are looking to find an idea you can develop into something profitable. You can jump from one deal to the next and enjoy the search for new opportunities. Things come and go. Nothing goes forever.

The time to think how to sell your business is when you start the business. Who will buy what you have created? Will you get a premium for your efforts?

Some argue you can make more money by starting a business and selling it than by holding a business and running it. For others, the fun of running something may give you cash flow and a lifestyle that will be hard to replace.

You start with the end in mind because you do not know what you do not know. You hedge your bet in case you got into a business you don't like.

Many discover too late that they built a business dependent on the owner of the business. When the owner is not involved, the business and value collapses. To sell a business, you design a plan that will run successfully without you involved.

Step #2. Do I Have a Niche?

Why should anyone buy your service or use your product? Why do I care? Why do I need this? Is it unique, does it exist? Is the market for my idea big enough to build a profitable business?

A good idea will stand up to the pressure of competition. Simply doing something is not enough if others are already doing it. Unless you can do it better, you may not be able to compete. Conceiving new, better and different is endless while following someone else's idea may simply lead to trouble.

A niche is anything that gives you an edge over the competition. The stronger the niche, the better the chances are it will prove successful. A niche may be real or it may be a marketing concept that gives the perception of being unique. If you cannot describe why your idea is a better idea, do you think someone will buy your idea? Start thinking about a niche with research.

Technology and communications have made researching ideas easy using the internet. Some information is not worth the screen you see it on, check the sources of information. However, the more you research ideas, the more confidence you can develop. You may find you have something you can work with.

My Dad had a horse as big as a Clydesdale in the early 1940's. He had an idea and met with a local dairy farmer. He convinced the farmer to give him a home delivery route. The idea became an instant success as kids told their moms to buy milk from the man with the horse and wagon. Everyone else was delivering milk in trucks; the niche was delivering milk by horse and wagon.

Wally "Famous" Amos started with a simple cookie recipe and an idea. He built a cookie empire with entertainment marketing. Famous Amos himself became the niche and people associated him with his cookies. He marketed his chocolate chip cookies as an entertainer with his Hawaiian shirts and big Panama hats. Wally was not the only one with a good chocolate chip cookie recipe; his niche was unique marketing. It made him rich and famous.

Established companies may get fat, lazy and become a target. A restaurant may have allowed service to get sloppy. Or it may be a marketing company that got to the top as a "One Trick Pony" and can no longer produce hot ideas.

Companies and services may start like a ball of fire but stop paying attention to details. Big companies may let you get away with beating them in one unique area as long as you do not hurt them materially. Moreover, big companies may not have the time or may simply overlook a small opportunity. However, a small opportunity for a big company may be a huge business opportunity for you.

Focus on a unique position that you can develop. Finding a niche is your edge. Be sure your plan starts out with a good reason why it is going to be a winner.

Step #3. Am I Using Leverage?

Find a successful business and you will see leverage. Leverage is anything that extends you, your experience, your knowledge, your ideas, or your business. People are the ultimate leverage and the most important part of any venture. You hire and train people to work your ideas. You want them to learn, grow, and eventually replace yourself. That is how you create leverage.

Systems are advantageous and may be as important as the idea. Systems provide you with ways to duplicate ideas successfully. Come up with a system that works and you many have a business.

Marketing is leverage. A message that motivates people to buy your product or service is like having a salesperson making a call for you. If you are a good marketer with the right product or service, you can build a brand. A brand is leverage. Brands create loyalty, insure repeat business, and may bring higher prices. People will pay more for perceived value.

You can outsource your ideas to others; your suppliers are leverage to your business. Pay others to do things for you more efficiently than you can do yourself. Leverage makes a business virtually unlimited to any size or scope.

Step #4 Who Is On My Team?

No one is an island. It will be hard, if not impossible, to create success without help. No one has all the skill sets and talent. At the very least, you need legal advice and financial support.

Entrepreneurs have a reputation for being good with ideas and innovation but little skills or desire to run a business. That is true in some cases because many entrepreneurs enjoy the chase and starting a business. They would rather sell the business to others and start something new. Others however, start ideas and stay with them for a lifetime. They become stewards of their creations.

From the very beginning, you may have to come up with a way to share equity in your venture. You may have to offer the ability to earn equity as the business grows to attract key people.

Step #5. How Do I Reach and Sell Customers?

A successful business gets new customers faster than it loses them. It is a principle of attrition. You cannot satisfy everyone no matter what you do. As long as you add more customers than you lose, you can grow a business. That will take a sales effort and marketing. If you are one of those people who hate sales, change that thinking.

Business cannot survive without sales and marketing. As a creator and leader of the venture, master the concept of sales and marketing.

Sales generate cash. Who cares about a hot idea if you cannot sell a product, service or make it profitable? Define how your product will be sold and how you will make people aware of your service, product, or idea.

Step #6. Does My Idea Pass The Acid Test?

Do this plan for a reason. You want the results to get you free, independent and wealthy. The plan should be a business or venture that you can work ON but not IN.

Many business owners discover after years of effort their business never grew or made enough money to get them to their goals. They eventually wound up selling or closing the business and going back to a job to get a paycheck.

They personally become so integral to the day-to-day operations they never took time to work on the business and make it grow.

> **Are You Starting A Business Or Venture That Will Make You Rich Or Are You Creating A Job For Yourself?**

The plan from the very beginning should lead you, as the owner and creator, to work ON the business. The job of the entrepreneur is to make the business or venture a success, not to be a worker in the business. If you are thinking of doing something so small it will only support you, it is not a business, it is being self-employed.

You cannot run a car dealership if you are on the showroom floor selling cars. Wayne Huizenga may have started driving a garbage truck but that was never his intention after he got the business started. Bill Gates started Microsoft but it was never his idea to be a programmer. The General directs the army but does not get in the fight.

Many people are so frustrated with a job or dead end career they will try anything to get freedom and independence. However, a business or venture that owns your time may turn into a nightmare. When you design a plan, your goal is to own the business, not BE the business.

A business does not stand still. It is either going up or it is going down. In business, you may be doing fine until you have a direct competitor and that may change everything. That is why you want to be moving ahead, not staying even. Growing the business is not just for the money, it is for protection of the business.

An entrepreneur is flexible. They start out looking for opportunity but may not personally be concerned with managing and leading. However, shortsighted quick-buck artist thinking leads to sloppy ideas with plans full of holes. Start with the best intentions of long-term success of a business whether you are a long-term player or not.

Putting a Real Business Plan Together

If you think your test plan can work and you are ready to put a real plan together, a great place to start is the U.S. Government Small Business Administration web site at http://www.sba.gov. This is a web site with a wealth of information. It covers writing business plans, copyrights, financing, and how to borrow money.

Before computers, writing and putting a formal business plan together was not only tedious work, you had to create and design what you wanted to accomplish.

Creating a formal business plan is faster, easier, and professional with the help of inexpensive software. Business Plan programs designed by experienced business professionals will help lead you to key questions and problems that need to be answered in virtually any business situation. The final product from a good software program will give you a professional looking presentation.

Business planning software covers financial projections, cash flow forecasting, strategy, sales, and marketing. While no software program can do all things for you, planning software will save you endless hours of time and give you a professional edge.

The way to get people excited about your ideas is not to talk about *what you think will work*, but to show others *how it will work*. Business people listen to ideas, *but respond to data and well designed plans*.

If you are confident about your ideas, create a formal business plan and in the process, you will learn more. Ideas are like journeys, they start with a first step. A plan is the first step. If you do a plan enough times, you improve with experience and the plan may become real.

What About the Money?

"I don't have the money, how can I get in business." That roadblock is inexperience. Getting started is not about the money, it is about making a good idea work.

Many ideas get started with $20,000 or less and come from people who have never been a manager or run a business. Business is not rocket science; it is creating good systems to make ideas profitable.

When it comes to money, there is no scarcity of money! There is only a scarcity of good ideas and people to make things happen. If you have something that gets you excited, with a niche, have people in mind to help you, have the sales angle figured out and you can clearly see the results, then you can find the money. If your idea is good, money will chase it.

We have a strong economy and many people with money looking for a place to invest. You attract people and money with opportunity and a good return on investment.

Investors and people betting on you will want solid evidence you know what you are doing. A plan with a team of people to make it work is what venture capitalists want to see and what a banker may be willing to bet on.

Get ideas started and be sure they have the critical elements to be successful. The formality of getting started does not matter as much as thinking opportunity and success.

Rich and Free
Entrepreneur's Guide

- Plans are blueprints for action.
- Don't judge others, profit from them.
- Ideas mean little without a system that works and makes money.
- Do a plan, test your ideas.
- There is no scarcity of money, only ideas and people to make plans work.

Chapter 7

Leadership: Getting Others to Follow

Don't tell people how to do things, tell them what to do and let them surprise you with their results.
—George S. Patton

Play Backwards

Rugby is distinguished from football; the ball can only be passed backwards. The object of the fast-moving game is to win points by carrying, passing, kicking and grounding the ball.

There is no stopping for time outs, limited substitutions and no pads. Rough tackles mean no wimps allowed. Ball control is by brute force. If you are averse to copious amounts of pain, this a game you watch, not a game you play. You could call rugby elegant violence. You can also call rugby a study in entrepreneurial leadership.

Only the fittest survive where deficiencies are quickly exposed. The variation of skills and physical requirements means there is opportunity for individuals of every shape, size and ability...as long as you have the courage.

If you are a leader, you get out of your own way in order to move forward. It's a hard lesson for some to learn, many do not want others to score. They want to be the winner and score all the points themselves.

Managers get power from hoarding information without sharing it, they hold on to the ball. They wonder why teammates don't like to play with them. People work for managers because they have to. Managers who do not learn how to play the game stay as managers, they don't become leaders.

Leaders grow people. They pass the ball and they help others. They have a vision on how to win the game. Leaders get things done through others by helping them grow. Leaders and entrepreneurs move up the ladder because the people who work for them, help push them up. People want to work for leaders.

The hierarchal adversarial relationship management system has long dominated business in America. Managers who adapt to the new rules of business and think like entrepreneurs become the long-term winners. The name of the game is to get to the goal. Everyone is a player in the game.

Creating Wealth Is A Team Sport

You need the help of like-minded people. Others that help you may have different personalities and viewpoints and that is an advantage. However, people need to share the leader's visions and be running at the same goals.

Entrepreneurs do not need warm bodies around them simply to get things done. They need people who think creatively and put innovation to work.

The secret to leadership is understanding how others are motivated and to use this knowledge as a strategy. This insight helps get things done efficiently. Knowing why people do things is a strategic advantage. You avoid problems when you have players around you that are working towards the same goals.

Creating wealth and getting rich is not an emotional experience, it is about using intellect. Making money is about using your brains and avoiding a big catastrophic mistake or loss that may set you back for years.

People are Different

Everyone has unique backgrounds, viewpoints, cultures, and experiences. People see things from their perspective, not yours.

What we understand about motivation is it drives all of us. However, it's important to understand the principles why you cannot drive other people's motivations or change their values. People understand motivation from their perspective; it's what works for them. You cannot assume your motivation will work for others.

The way to motivate people is to create an environment for the situation. People in the right environment, with the right incentive, will motivate themselves. Adjust your attitude towards others and do not expect others to adjust to you. Treat all people differently. Everyone is a unique individual.

Motivation Principles:

1. *All* People Are Motivated

2. You *Can't* Motivate Other People

3. People Do Things For Their Reasons, *Not Your Reasons*

4. A Person's Strength Overused May Become Their Weakness

5. The Very Best One Can Do To Motivate Others Is To *Create An Environment* That Allows Specific Individuals To Motivate Themselves

Leadership Is Not Crowd Control

Understanding motivation principles allows you to create environments that strong-minded and creative people can work in. Environments allow people to take ownership of what they do.

People follow leaders they trust. The distinction between leadership and management is trust, not envy, or control.

Corporate and entrepreneurial leadership skills are different because the job is different. Layers of management, political agendas, and a unique culture mean success in a corporation may have little to do with success of the company. Corporate leaders are sensitive to company politics in order to get things accomplished.

Entrepreneurs seek opportunity. Their motivation is pride of winning, excitement of accomplishment. The rewards are wealth and riches.

Entrepreneurial leaders develop a style that will get them to the goal. That means allowing others to win as well. The successful entrepreneur knows the biggest resource is people, so they put people first. People bring ideas, creativity, and innovation and that helps new ventures topple old ones.

Managers and Leaders do it Different

Managers supervise. They rely on operating skills, organizational ability and use power, authority and resources to achieve the organizational goals. The job is to be sure employees get things done right with efficiency. Managers solve problems and create policies.

Entrepreneurs develop visions, use business insight, and rely on communication and people skills. They empower others to get results. They look for opportunities to do things better through innovation and creativity.

Entrepreneurs tend to have less formal arrangements of the decision making and supervision process. The difference between leaders and managers is style. People with confidence deal directly and openly with problems and are not afraid to make people angry when making an unpopular decision.

Skills of Entrepreneurial Leaders:

Thick Skin and Courage

Like the pioneers in the old west, leaders are in front of the pack and often are mistaken for the enemy. They are shot in the back. It takes courage to stay with a plan and vision that has not materialized. Leaders do not lose sight of where they are going and believe what they are doing is right and stay the course.

Priority

Entrepreneurs have vision and a sense of priority. They look for an edge and focus on the big picture.

They filter out the day-to-day distractions and the "noise" of operations.

Horse Sense

Horse sense has little to do with intelligence; it's an intuitive skill developed from experience.

Active Listening Skills

Leaders are active listeners and pay attention. They seek quality information and insight to make decisions and draw conclusions but not to gain consensus. Advice from people with real life successful experience is valued above all others as entrepreneurs seek accomplished people in their fields.

Mistakes - Part of the Game

Mistakes are a part of taking risks, correcting them quickly is essential.

Build the Best Team

Find the best talent that is like-minded and have similar goals. Reward performance with material incentives and go to extremes to establish creative environments.

A Positive Attitude

A passionate and positive attitude is infectious. Entrepreneurs focus on individuals and are quick to compliment others.

Communication Experts

Entrepreneurs need to be able to influence others and sell concepts. A good sense of humor breaks the ice and eases situations. Inspire others with passion, good communicators use humility to make fun of themselves and project as real people.

Think Strategically

The general who wins the battle make many calculations in his temple before the battle is fought. The general who loses makes but few calculations before hand.

—**Sun Tzu**

Entrepreneurs are intuitively street smart and savvy, plan well, think strategically and as a rule, don't make emotional decisions. They calculate and run scenarios of what can happen, both good and bad, and see problems and obstacles as part of doing business. They try to anticipate problems and focus on the big picture.

Integrity Is Everything

Leaders respect and value people above all other assets. Developing trust and keeping integrity is everything. The number one reason people follow leaders is trust. Keep your word and do not break promises.

One Thing Leads to Another

Think one thing and something else comes of it. And sometimes it is something unexpected. R. Buckminster Fuller called it precession and it affects bodies in motion on *other* bodies in motion. The principle repeats itself over and over in nature, science, and business. It's doing things and thinking one-way that leads you to another.

One of the principles of precession is when you start something new it may create other opportunities. You may discover things only because you have taken action or started something new.

Precession

Bees and flowers are a metaphor to show how this works. The honeybee finds flowers and crawls inside. The bee is after the nectar to make honey. However, in the process, the bee is dusted with pollen. As the bee moves on to the next flower for more nectar, it is cross-pollinating another flower. The bee thinks the job is to gather honey. However, the *purpose* is to pollinate flowers.

Another example of precession is Apple computer. They had been in the computer and software business since the 1970s long before it created the iPod music player and iTunes software. Someone was awake and thinking out of the box and saw an opportunity to get in the music industry. Apple developed the new hardware and software to both play music and get music royalties from downloading songs. Just because Apple was in the computer and software business, it did not stop them from thinking and doing something new. The iPod was a precessional effect; the thinking came from something Apple was already doing. It just took them in a different direction and Apple, again, reinvented itself.

David Saperstein was General Manager of a car dealership in Baltimore, Maryland when we first started doing business. I traded lease cars with David for radio station advertising. It was a win/win proposition. However, David saw a new way to trade advertising time with radio stations.

Rush hour was awful and people tied up in traffic jams had little real-time information how to avoid the problems. It would be a major benefit to radio stations if listeners could hear live traffic reports. So David founded Metro Traffic, a news and information company that supplied live traffic reports to radio stations without the sky-high costs of the radio station maintaining helicopters and airplanes. Metro Traffic was trading live information for radio station advertising. The new and unique concept grew Metro Traffic into a phenomenal nationwide success with precessional thinking.

The entrepreneur uses expertise to get things done through others. Winning is game, the report card is the money. They lead and inspire others to be as good as they can be. The reward for workers who create value is not just to keep a job; it's to share in the wealth.

It's the opposite of corporate thinking where the wealth is concentrated at the top ranks. Entrepreneurs reward contributors because that is their vision. They do not get into a business or venture because it's a hobby or fun to do, they focus on success and the rewards.

The entrepreneur's goal is to make the task rewarding for workers so they will not only work hard, but also be willing to contribute with new ideas and innovation.

Entrepreneurs approach the game as a team effort. As a company grows, it evolves and becomes more structured and political. The goals change and the players in the company assume different roles and become less connected to the immediate success.

Downside to Success and Intelligence: You Can Outsmart Yourself

It happens all too often, the successful hit the ceiling of success and blow up a good thing. It takes skill to start something and it takes just as much skill to keep success going. If you let success go to your head, you become complacent, overconfident and you lose your edge.

Signs of Leaders That Lost Their Way:

- Instead of helping others feel needed and important, they assume that role themselves, use sarcasm and cryptic remarks to keep others in line.

- They tell people how smart they are.

- They play favorites and downplay those that do not totally agree with them.

- They don't express gratitude for the help others give them.

- They become poor listeners.

- They started the business or venture and fell in love with their own creation. They lose objectivity.

- They don't have a second or third idea, they didn't think they needed one.

- They defend bad decisions instead of asking for help.

- They rely on the idea and not on the business of running the business.

The sign of real leadership is the ability to have others become part of the success, not in spite of it. Entrepreneurs who take advantage of people do not understand leadership principles and the importance of an aligned team of players

I have managed in big corporations and led small entrepreneurial companies. It's easy to understand why bureaucracy gets in the way of creativity and innovation.

In corporations, as you work up to the top of empires, layers of management become blockades and fortress of protection for turf. People block ideas and others from getting ahead of them. The incentive for many is not for the company to be more successful and make more profits, it's to protect their jobs and positions.

Entrepreneurial companies do not limit people because of title or position. A good idea is a good idea and if it makes money and creates success, the founder of the idea is likely to be in on the success and have monetary rewards.

Understanding motivation is how you lead others to greatness. It takes time and experience to make money. Entrepreneurs cannot afford to fall into the trap of being a manager who does not lead but makes rules and laws. That kills the entrepreneurial spirit and potential.

The final thought is about chasing only the money. Rewards come to leaders and entrepreneurs who use intelligence and do the right things. The wealth in leadership comes in creating excellence in people who help you create wealth. Putting money ahead of good business practices may lead to short-term gains but long-term problems.

Leaders are the assets of a business venture, leaders are critical to success. Many venture capitalists will only bet on the people involved and skip opportunities if they feel the management team is not right for the job.

Creating something may bring problems and good leaders are problem solvers. They know how to fix things and they can make things work. A good business does not happen because of ideas, it happens because people make the ideas work.

People are the wealth, not the business. Many have ideas and information but few know how to turn it into wealth or make money with it. That is the job of the entrepreneurial. They inspire others to create success.

A top-notch entrepreneur never stops learning as a business will not stand still. Be at the leading edge or you may not survive a competitive battle. Hire the best, let others play in the game and lead like a hero. People around you will let you get to the goal and they will help push you forward.

Rich and Free Entrepreneur's Guide

1. You can't lead top notch players with a hierarchal management style.
2. People will help you get rich and wealthy if they are in the game.
3. Share the wealth: getting rich is a team sport.
4. Understand motivation principles: it's the key to successful leadership.
5. Precession happens: keep looking for the new opportunities.

Chapter 8

We Are All Salespeople!

Understand that you need to sell you and your ideas in order to advance your career, gain more respect, and increase your success, influence, and income. The fact is, everyone is in sales. Whatever area you work in, you do have clients and you do need to sell.

—**Jay Abraham**

Sales generate income. Income creates cash flow. Cash flow leads to profits. Without profits, you have no business.

Hot and Muggy

I cut lawns in high school to make lunch money. I had steady customers and an old lawn mower. I was making a little over two dollars an hour and if I hustled, I could make enough money to have some left over for the weekend.

I was hitchhiking to school as I did every day when a man stopped to give me a ride.

"Get in," he said, "where are you going?"

I told him Coral Gables High. He said that was on his way and he would drop me off in front of school.

"I'm on my way to work. I'm a salesman and I sell Fuller Brushes," he said.

The salesman didn't seem that much older than me, I asked, "How old do you have to be to get a job in that company?"

He said, "Well, you're too young to get hired. But if you want to make some spending money, come and work for me. You can sell on my route; I have a big territory to cover. Saturdays are a good day for sales and you won't be in school. I'll teach you how to sell and I'll pay you a commission on any orders you can get."

"Ok, I'll try it," I said on the spot, I had little to lose. Anything was better than cutting lawns in the heat; even door-to-door sales had to be easier.

Saturday came around and the salesman picked me up at my house. We drove to his sales territory in Hialeah. On the way, he told me what to do and how to sell. It was not very complicated.

"It's simple," said the salesman.

"Go to every house on the block and don't skip any. If someone answers the door at the house, offer them a free potato and veggie scrubber. If they take the scrubber, ask if you can come inside and show them what you have to sell," he continued.

"Once you get inside the house, the chances are you can sell something. Just talk slow and be nice, nothing to it," he said. He was convincing and made it sound easy enough.

Potato and veggie scrubber in one hand, sample case in the other, I walked up to a door and knocked. A woman answered.

I told her I was from Fuller Brush and asked if I could show here some things. I offered her the free scrubber. She looked down on me and said in a gruff voice, "How old are you?"

I said I was almost 17 and going to high school. She invited me in and patiently let me show her everything I had in the sample case. When I finished, I asked if she would like to buy anything.

"Yes," she said. My first call and I made a sale.

She ordered cleaning brushes, hairbrushes and a stove cleaning brush. I left the house and thought, one more sale like this and I would have made as much money as I could cutting a lawn. I was able to sell about thirty percent of the people who answered the door.

At the end of the day, I met the salesman and my new boss. I showed him my orders.

"If you can sell like this every Saturday, you can buy a scooter for yourself. You won't have to hitchhike to school," he said.

I knew at my age, I did not know very much. However, I was smart enough to figure out it wasn't hard work. The key to sales was how fast could I get to the next house and make another call.

More Sales Jobs, More Learning

After graduating high school, I got a service technician job fixing copy machines. Part of my job was to sell service contracts and paper supplies. For everything I sold, I was paid a commission on top of my salary. I worked hard at getting my customers to buy service agreements. I sold so many supplies and service agreements I was promoted to full time sales.

By the time I was twenty-four I was a sales supervisor in midtown New York City teaching a team how to sell copy machines. However, I wanted a more creative job so I took a position selling directory advertising in the fashion and garment industry.

I learned how to write advertising copy and came up with sales and marketing ideas for clients. It was enough to earn me a job at *Women's Wear Daily* newspapers and later a job at *Mademoiselle Magazine*.

From print advertising sales, I went into broadcast and radio sales. At the age of thirty, I became General Manager of a radio station in Baltimore thanks to my success in sales. Selling gave me independence and opened the door to management.

Understanding Others

Selling taught me important lessons about filling needs and helping others. Learning how a business grew and became more successful was my first-hand business education. In order to sell to clients, I had to help them. I had to learn how their business operated. The more I learned about business, the more successful and easier it was to sell advertising.

The most successful business people I met were the ones that considered marketing and sales the key part of their business. I called on hundreds of businesses, sold millions of dollars in advertising, and was seeing the same story repeatedly. The most successful businesses were the ones that focused on sales and marketing. The priority of selling was as important as the business itself.

By the time I got into management, I was able to draw on what I learned. I had a good idea how to create marketing plans from my experience helping others and I knew the important things to focus on in business.

I met people from different backgrounds. Many had little to do with sales and marketing and a lot of them did not like salespeople. They thought selling was a second rate way of making a living. To them, selling was something "others" could handle.

Sales People and Lawyers Share an Image

The overwhelming odds are as a businessperson or entrepreneur, you will find yourself dealing with sales and marketing.

Sales people and lawyers share the same stigma. It's a negative perception and the media and Hollywood magnify it. Both the legal profession and professional sales are in the business of influence and persuasion and that attracts attention, both good and bad.

Lawyers get a bad rap for being self-serving and unscrupulous. Much like in the sales field, most people in the legal field work hard at helping others. However, the image of one bad lawyer may be enough to make all lawyers appear to be the low life of professionals.

People don't like sales because of the image or an experience. An aggressive or rude salesperson can turn anyone off. Regardless of the stigma, everyone sells something. At some time or another, we all sell our ideas and ourselves.

Ask the CEO or President of a business to describe their job and you will likely hear,

"I am the chief salesman. I make things happen."

Sales are important to entrepreneurs and business people for a simple enough reason:

> **Nothing Happens Until Someone Sells Something**

Selling is the ability to influence others. To *get* to the top of a business, be a good communicator. That means learning how to sell yourself and your ideas.

Selling is not rocket science and it's easy enough to learn the basics. You do not have to be a pro to understand the process. Sales skills will make you a better businessperson and a more accomplished entrepreneur.

Marketing is a Mind Game

People without first-hand experience tend to lump sales and marketing skills together but they are very different and require different skills.

Selling something is a transaction. You sell something and someone buys something. Selling evolves around the customer. To better sell yourself and sell products, understand how others see things. Their point of view is more important than your point of view. The sales job is to learn what others need. Every business needs different tactics and strategies to sell their product or service.

Marketing is about creating perception, image, or feelings in the mind. Marketing is the process of trying to influence others perceptions. When you market a product or service, you are setting up a pre-condition to make something happen or assist in sales. Marketing creates awareness and starts the sales process. It makes selling easier and more effective.

> **Marketing Positions A Product Or Service In The Mind Of The Customer**

Marketing principles work in careers as well. By changing how others perceive your behavior and attitude, you may be able to re-position how others value your time, service, and contribution. Leaders work at becoming a brand in order to separate themselves and elevate their position. Marketing helps create brands and brand awareness.

A brand identifies items or services and differentiates them from competitors. A brand implies a pledge of satisfaction and quality.

If you try to sell something, that has no brand identity, the customer has no way to perceive or evaluate the product or service, *except for the price*. When people are aware or influenced by marketing, the perception may create an opportunity to sell products faster at higher prices.

Marketing accomplishes something else. It helps repeat sales. I learned a marketing principle when I called on a media buyer in Detroit that placed advertising for Chevrolet cars nationwide. She told me advertising was not only to sell cars. The advertising was a form of long-term product reinforcement. People who see the marketing of a car they are driving makes them feel better about the buying decision they made.

Sales skills create wealth. These skills may not be the first thing on your list of what you need to learn but you may have to change your priorities.

People have to know you are in business and they need to know what you do. Authors need readers, business needs customers, car washes need cars, and politicians need people. Everything in business runs on sales and marketing in some form or another.

> **Selling And Marketing Is The Trade Of Understanding The Needs Of Others.**

A banker will be hard-pressed to lend you money and it will be difficult to convince a venture capitalist to invest in your business without persuasive abilities.

If your image of selling or marketing is a profession or field below your education, this thinking may be enough to stop you from considering being an entrepreneur. Sales and marketing may not be your favorite business activity but at the very least, do not view it negatively.

One of the reasons I was successful at improving radio stations was I never let go of the marketing and sales strategies. That was the key strength to the business. It's what I studied and learned how to master.

When you underestimate others, it's arrogance and it may become ignorance. When you are not concerned what others may do, it will take the edge off your thinking. Fear and competition keep you sharp. Use fear to become stronger, *not more worried.*

> *Only the paranoid survive.*
> —**Andy Grove,** *CEO Intel*

Products and Services Don't Stand Still

Even the worst products can improve if they stay in business long enough. Nothing stands still. The way to keep moving ahead is to improve what you do and improve the image through advertising, marketing and sales.

> **The Distinction Of A Product Or Service May Be So Small It Cannot Be Measured Except For The Perception In The Mind Of The Customer!**

Perception in a competitive business is the difference between winning and losing. In a close horse race, the quality or difference in the product or service may not be enough to win. It may come down to superior marketing and selling strategies.

Proven Rules:

1. Success or failure in business may have less to do with the product or service and more to do with sales and marketing.

2. Learn how to influence others. Learn how to be a better communicator. Entrepreneurs must be able to sell themselves and their ideas in order to lead others.

3. Customers *are* the business. Sales and marketing is the lifeline to success. Focus on what it takes to hold customers and add new ones.

> **Learn Why People Make Decisions And Why People Do The Things That They Do.**

Rich and Free Entrepreneur's Guide

- Selling is a transaction.
- Marketing creates perception.
- Nothing happens in business until someone sells something.
- Salespeople have an image as bad as lawyers do and that is someone else's problem. Do not make it your problem.

Part 2

Why People
Get Stuck

Fear of failure is often more damaging than failure itself. Fear incapacitates unsuccessful people. What stops most people from success is lack of drive, education, and skills.

Chapter 9

The Roadblocks of Risk and Fear

Avoiding danger is no safer in the long run than outright exposure. The fearful are caught as often as the bold.
Helen Keller
Deafblind Author and Activist

It's easy to quarterback a play after you have seen it. You have perfect hindsight, it's 20/20 vision in the rear view mirror. However calling a play is not easy. That is why good quarterbacks get paid big bucks. Once the play starts, spontaneous, unpredictable things happen.

That is what life is, spontaneously unpredictable. You may have knowledge, a good education and a great attitude but you still have to adjust your game plan to real time. Nothing teaches lessons better than real life. You learn from your experience or you learn from others. However we learn lessons or get information, the knowledge we acquire helps us plan our future.

Of course planning is a risk because you do not experience the future. You anticipate the future. How you see the future is in your mind, what you do depends on how of you think. You are either a proactive doer or a reactive looker.

The past helps your future planning but in no way predicts the future. If your attitude is optimistic and you are strong willed, the past helps you. Overcoming adversity gives you character and strength. However, if you have little self-confidence, bad experiences may leave you feeling hopeless.

> **Experiences, Good Or Bad,
> Guide Your Future.**

If you are thinking you "Shudda, Cudda, Wudda," it is time to think what you are going to do about it. You get one life; you get one silver bullet in the gun.

You Can't Re-Run the Play

If you screw up your life because you didn't take the shot, it's not like instant sports replays on TV. You do not get to rewind the tape and do the play over again. You did whatever you did to yourself. Even if outside forces and things happened to you, it is your choice how you deal with things. Life is not only about what happens to you, it's about how you react to things that happen to you.

The time it takes to reach your goals is not throwaway time. Time is the one thing you never get back. You do not get to your goals and suddenly get happy because you reached them. Success is a process. The journey to your goals *is* your life. Many discover the chase of going after goals was the best thing that happened to them.

You have to assess what you want and what are your priorities.

DO YOU:
Want freedom?
Want to get rich?
Want to enjoy what you do?
Want control of your career?
Want to have something to pass on to your kids?
Want to max the potential of your education and skills?
Hate being told what to do!
Don't like being told what you're worth!
Don't want to take 30 years to get wealthy!

Most people agree with these ideas not just because of the money, it is about being free. Freedom, however, has a price. The word freedom does not in any way imply it is free. The question is: What is freedom going to cost me?

Making a decision to do something and actually doing something are different things. When you start on a path to do something, you have a better image of yourself. Your self-esteem improves.

People who care about you will pay attention when you take action. Having a goal and a mission gives you a reason to get out of bed in the morning; you look forward to something you control.

Choices to Create Wealth

1. **Work for others, earn wages, less risk: Twenty or thirty year timeframe to create enough wealth for freedom.**

2. Work for yourself as an entrepreneur: Create your own income, more risk, greater potential, unlimited riches.

The way to get rich while working for others is dependent on how you spend your money and how you invest. Money working for you will be the key to your long-term success.

While you do not have to take extreme risks to grow money, be aggressive about planning your money. Compound interest grows at a faster rate as your savings and investments grow. Over a twenty or thirty year period, you can create millions on relatively modest wages. Be willing to save and invest to take advantage of compound interest.

The other way to get rich is to work for yourself as an entrepreneur. The wealth you can create is unlimited. However, it is impossible to calculate how long it may take to create wealth. You may do one good deal and retire on that alone. You can set up a business that will provide you with passive income so time is yours even while your business grows.

Many venture capitalists will not invest in a venture unless it meets a 35% annual growth rate. That kind of return can easily get you in and out of a business in five years or less. In one good deal or business venture, you may be able to earn a lifetime of income. As a rule of thumb, five years is a barometer of a successful business venture. However, that can vary wildly.

As an entrepreneur, you are on your own how to handle taxes and your money. You should have professional advice to maximize your income. As a business or owner in a business, you will have many tax and investment options over a worker earning wages. A successful business or venture will create happy problems.

Working for others or doing it on your own, the key to success will be your financial literacy. Become smart about your money. The rich and wealthy are not necessarily the most educated. However, what they have in common is an understanding of money and good habits.

At a job, your work contributes to the value of the company. However, you own none of the company and you have no equity. Your future is not about your current job and income. Your future is about the choices you make to save, invest, and grow your future. You create your own equity.

> **You Choose To Create Wealth,
> It Is Not A Coin Flip.**

Getting rich is a lifetime process. Know yourself and work on overcoming limitations that hold you back. It means learning specialized skills directly related to creating wealth. Acquire specialized knowledge to create success.

It takes a burning desire and passion to go on a path most people avoid. That is why people are not millionaires and wealthy. They are not confident they have the personality, skills, or knowledge to pull it off.

> **Risk Of Failure and Lack Of Specialized Education
> Keeps Things Status Quo.**

There is absolutely no doubt entrepreneurs can earn many times more than an employee, and in fact, there is no limit to what they can earn if they control the deals or the company. This is why entrepreneurs are getting more notice and recognition. They are the ones to make things happen and drive the economy.

Where Are You?

A job in itself is a short-term answer to a long-term problem. If you are young and starting out, you have little vested in a job. The odds are you have not acquired real assets and have little to lose. You cannot risk what you do not have. Many feel the best time to try to do something is while you are young, with little responsibility, commitment and expenses.

If you are mid-stream in life, you may have a family and children. You may have accumulated expenses and have real assets to protect. If things are going along well, you may need to stay put. But if your are at midlife and about to hit the peak earning years and see little upside, your risk is you may spend your entire life working and not reach your goals or potential.

A decision to risk your current situation, if you have something of value, is a hard call. Be realistic about your situation and your future prospects. A job or simply getting along is little more than putting in time. You have to decide how you want to spend the rest of your time. What are you willing to risk?

Why People Fail or Get Stuck At The Bottom:

1. **Fear of failure.**
2. **Afraid of change.**

3. Not willing to take a risk.
4. Ignorance (not lack of education or intelligence).
5. No specialized knowledge of skills that create wealth.
6. Lack of passion, drive or initiative.
7. Poor communication skills, can't sell themselves or their ideas.
8. No mentor or mastermind group to help with ideas and encouragement.
9. Not willing to take charge of their own careers.

Pain and Pleasure

Two things motivate people, pain, and pleasure. Pain is more powerful than pleasure. People will do about anything to avoid pain; the fear of failure incapacitates unsuccessful people. The pain and pleasure principle is well known. People are driven to pleasure and avoid pain. In other words, they will do things that bring pleasure and unwilling to do things that cause pain. It guides virtually everything we do, whether we are aware of it or not.

Logic Gets Overruled

The paradox is the emotions and physical reality of pain and pleasure are out of balance. Most people agree the drive to avoid pain is stronger than the drive to seek pleasure.

Many times our thinking is not rational and this is partly because of our biological survival system. We automatically avoid any source of pain. We know the difference between physical and emotional pain, yet we still have trouble distinguishing the two. In the end, logic is overruled, and most people react to real and perceived pain the same way.

People self-limit themselves and do not achieve a fraction of what they are capable of achieving because of the fear of failure. Fear creates a self-fulfilling prophecy. People do not allow themselves success because the fear of failure is simply too much pain.

When we are young, we are more apt to seek pleasure. The young worry less about immediate problems, costs, or pain as long as the pleasure is worth the effort. It is the rationality of youth and strength. This is why many young people start their own businesses. They have little fear. If they do fail, it is not a big deal.

However, the same 23 year old at age 45 will be more conservative and less willing to take chances. Our risk tolerance decreases with age.

Understanding this principle and applying it is crucial to success. If you have a successful discipline, you can overcome the fears. The fact is, in almost every situation, people would rather be rich and wealthy than middle class or poor. What holds them back is not that they do not want the pleasure of freedom and independence that riches bring, it's they are more afraid of failure.

Many get over the fear of failure when a job or career suddenly ends. The risk of failure to try something new is less; they now have little to lose. However, many hang on to bogus jobs. They know what they are doing offers little income and even less security but fear holds them back. They do not do anything about the problem until they forced into action. Many times, that action simply never happens.

It is no secret. People get in a rut, get lazy and secretly are just plain afraid. The way to solve the problem is to gain confidence. You get confidence with education. Learning new skills will solve career and money problems. With good financial education, you can create wealth and get rich. To get over fear, get educated and learn specialized skills.

A Helping Hand from the Government

One reason to consider the risk to become an entrepreneur is that while, it may be a harder road, it has advantages workers will never enjoy. A business has huge benefits over workers earning a paycheck. When you control a business, you are in control of how you pay your taxes. You legally can defer income and you can write off assets of your business. You can control your future and put back your earnings into growing your venture or business.

A business is a separate legal entity in the eyes of the law. If you personally go bankrupt and overextend yourself, you are responsible and you may be liable for that debt for years to come. However, a business properly set up may go bankrupt and you personally will have no liability. You may lose the business but you will not lose your home or personal assets and belongings. Professional accountants and legal advisors help you make decisions to protect yourself. It is an important reason people choose to own a business.

A Business Puts You in Control

Owning a business or entity has advantages aside from taxes and cash flow. As long as you can generate cash flow and make a profit, you will have income. You are in control, you make the decisions, and you have legal options and alternatives.

Businesses employs people and those people pay taxes. The government has incentive to help business and corporations continue to earn profits and keep the workers employed.

It is in government's interest that a business is successful. You will not learn or be aware of those advantages as a wage earner unless you take the time to educate yourself. When the help of legal and financial professionals, you will learn how the system works.

When you own some form of a company, you have joined the ranks of the privileged and much more control of your fate and your income.

Incomes have been flat for years while inflation keeps ticking up. Think how this will play out for you. The question of risk for reward is relative; it depends on your income and situation. If your income does not grow as fast or faster than inflation, the choice to continue what you are doing may become easier. If you get in a situation where you are starting to sink, you will need to learn how to swim in a hurry.

Necessity Is the Mother of Innovation

Many have jumped from jobs to being entrepreneurs when their jobs were lost or cut back.

Either way, if you decide to take the risk or stay at a job, you will have your work cut out for you. In both cases, work at becoming financially literate and understand money or you will be a slave to money forever.

No one forces you to do anything. You can do anything you want but keep in mind that the entitlement days are gone and they will not come back. You are on your own to make your fortune and you are virtually alone to make long-term plans and decisions about your retirement.

As we live longer and healthcare improves, people will have multiple careers. Many will think becoming an entrepreneur in their 60's is the prime of youth and the best time to start something new with all that experience. It is all in your perspective. How you think is everything. You need skills, knowledge, determination and you need to get over fear of failure.

Rich and Free Entrepreneur's Guide

1. You get one shot at life, no replays.
2. Are you thinking "Shudda, Cudda, Wudda?"
3. Fear of failure incapacitates unsuccessful people.
4. The less you have to risk, the easier it is to go for it.
5. Working for others is immediate income but a slow way to riches.
6. Entrepreneurs and business people get a helping hand from the government.

Part 3

Traditional Thinking Isn't Working Anymore

In today's world, not adjusting is not an option. We cannot afford to be complacent. The most important lesson is that structural changes have created fierce competition. We must adapt to new rules and ways of doing things.

Macroeconomic policies play a part in our lives as new players become increasingly powerful in the global economy. It means new, fast-growing sources of demand, and new opportunities. To realize personal gains, make the necessary adjustments to your thinking and your education.

Chapter 10

Think Rich
to Get Rich

Think First, Get Rich Later
—Ben Stein
Economist, Actor

Net worth is only a number; it's the "Cash Flow" that counts. Cash flow is not what you are personally worth and not the profit you make in a business. Cash flow is the difference between income and expenses. It's the money coming in and money going out of a business or your personal account. Cash flow is one of the most important parts of financial planning, it's how you pay bills and meet your debt. Lenders, creditors, real estate investors, and money planners use cash flow analysis.

I learned how to manage cash flow while operating broadcasting companies. We rarely looked at profits. We watched the cash flow. If the cash flow was good, the profits were not far behind. If you do not have enough money to pay bills, you have overestimated income or underestimated expenses.

People who do not see a cash shortage are not minding their money. They don't have a picture of how much money is coming in or going out. If you cannot estimate cash flow, you will have trouble estimating *how to spend money*.

Spending money from cash flow allows you to keep your savings and net worth. If you spend money from your savings, you run the risk of running out of money.

The wealthy rarely spend the principle or deplete their savings. They use money to make more money and use cash flow to buy luxuries and toys.

Managing money is the key to long-term planning and creating wealth. The goal is to create income-generating assets that support you. Being wealthy is not measured in how much your net worth is or how much money you have in the bank. You create wealth to gain freedom and independence. If you cannot manage your money and create assets to support you, you will never stop working.

How to Measure Wealth

> *...we can account wealth more precisely as the number of forward days for a specific number of people we are physically prepared to sustain at a physically stated time and space liberating level of metabolic and metaphysical regeneration. The amount of time you can live forward without working is the measure of wealth. In order to create wealth and become rich and free, you need a constant stream of cash flow.*
>
> **—Buckminster Fuller**
> Operating Manual For Spaceship Earth

Wealth is relative; it is not a specific amount. How long you can live in the future without working is how you define wealth. Wealth generates cash flow and cash flow gives you independence and freedom to do as you please.

People that do what they want when they want are wealthy. *However, you can make a lot of money and be rich but you may not be wealthy.*

If you make $500,000 a year income and have debt and expenses of $500,000, you are rich. However, you are also grinding away on the treadmill to keep money coming in to support the debt and expense. The secret to being wealthy is as simple as understanding 6th grade math. Wealth is the resource you control that will generate more cash flow than your expenses.

The "Rich get richer, and the poor get poorer" is true. The distinction between the rich and poor is the rich use cash flow to invest and spend. The poor spend their income and use debt to buy what they cannot afford. The rich get richer because they spend differently.

> **How To Spend Money Is As Important As The Ability To Make Money.**

Rich people use business principles for their personal finances. They manage their money as if they were a successful business. The rich have money work for them and use debt as leverage to make more money. The poor work for money, and have no passive income to help them.

If you invest in assets that grow and limit liabilities that depreciate, these habits over time can make you rich.

The Money Treadmill

In 1971 President Nixon took us off the Gold Standard. It was an effort to impose government management of economic policy and allowed the government deficit spending. As money was no longer pegged to the value of gold, the government could print as much money as it needed. The idea was to control inflation and the upwards wage-price spiral. The new economics of "fiat currency" became legal tender. The value of the dollar became a free-floating currency.

A Million Used to be Worth a Million

The government continues to print more and more money. As inflation moves higher, money depreciates. Over time, money buys less and less. The inherent value of paper money is zero. The value of paper currency is measured against the country printing the money. However, *fiat currency is not backed by anything but confidence.*

Inflation and the decreasing value of the dollar are why you need to make more money tomorrow than you make today. Your expenses will rise in the future. Making more and more money is not greed, *it's common sense.* You have to make more tomorrow *to stay even and keep up with the continuing deflation of the dollar.*

In 1971, a million dollars *was* worth a lot of money. You could buy a small mansion, exotic cars and you would have money left over. In 2006 you would need $5,015,867 to buy the same amount as a one million did in 1971.

Lottery winners, professional athletes and third and fourth-generation inheritors all face the same problem. If you don't learn how to manage your money, you may wind up bankrupt. It does not matter how much money you have or how rich you are. If you lack the skills to manage money, over time it can leave your hands.

To make smart money decisions, you need good information. With information and experience, you gain the knowledge. Quality information is priceless while much of the information we get is little more than data and advertising. Think for yourself and trust your judgment. No one is as concerned about your money as you are.

Properly Evasive

The government gives us information and tells us what is *in* the information. The problem is you need a master's degree in economics to *understand what the information is actually saying.*

Information may be "Properly Evasive." Put on your thinking cap! Government statistics, without a thorough understanding, may be as useful as reading a biased editorial. What we are told and what we know to be happening are two different things.

Money is adjusted by inflation. Inflation is a force we have little control over. You decide what you want to do with your money however *you do not decide what inflation does to your money.* Inflation is the most critical element we deal with in the economy and in our personal finances. The way to get ahead of inflation is to plan for it.

> **Inflation Is More Important**
> **In Long-Term Planning Than**
> **Interest Rates Going Up Or Down.**

One of the ways the government keeps the perception of inflation under control is underplaying the rising cost of our biggest assets, our homes. Most people have 50% of their net worth and equity tied up in home ownership.

When statistics roll out every month from the government about inflation, the Consumer Price Index (CPI) measures housing in what the government calls the "Owners Equivalent Rent." This is an attempt to calculate how much a home should rent for. The actual price inflation of homes is not included in the CPI calculations.

In spite of the fact that almost 70% of the U.S. is not renting but living in a home they own, the government measures the effective cost of rentals as an index of inflation. People who own homes do not pay rent. They own the house. That is the vast part of their net worth.

Housing in Los Angeles is an example of inflation. If you bought a home in 1975, it would likely have cost you $49,000. That home in 1985 appreciated to $125,000, $190,000 in 1995, and $575,000 in 2005. The average home price in Los Angeles over a 30-year period increased an average of $17,500 each year.

In 1975, the U.S. average income was $8,630 and a single wage earner paid approximately 5.6 times the annual income for a home. In 2005, the average home in Los Angeles cost 15.56 times the average U.S. income.

Inflation has gone up so much over time that the majority living in Los Angeles could not afford the house they live in if they had to buy their home at today's prices.

Debt-For-Diploma and Paycheck Paralysis

College graduates are earning less than graduates of 30 years ago. Real assets have increased with inflation while wages have stagnated. Earnings for workers with four-year degrees fell 5.2 percent between 2000 and 2004 when adjusted for inflation according to White House economists.

We are told people are not sharing equally in the economy because they do not have the right skills. But what is obvious is college graduate ranks are swelling and they face tougher competition for better-paying jobs.

It's a tough time to be young and entering the workforce. Many students have figured out college is becoming less of a stepping stone and more of a holding pen as tuitions have risen to staggering costs. The college ROI, (Return on Investment) does not look anywhere near as good as it did years ago.

New Times, New Rules

We have an economy like the 2,000-pound elephant and the 10-pound monkey. If you average the weight of the monkey and the weight of the elephant, you have a 1,000-pound monkey and 1,000-pound elephant. We have more people with more money than ever and more people with less money than ever and a shrinking middle class.

Not everyone is in the same financial situation. Your age, where you live and if inflation has been working for you or against you have everything to do with your income and net worth. The press reminds us that we are in troubling economic times.

U.S. standard of living is falling. We're all worse off than 25 years ago

It takes two workers to maintain a typical family lifestyle.

Today's children may become the first generation that won't live as well as their parents.

The United States is falling behind as other nations grow faster.

Bad news sells newspapers and makes good news copy. The good news that is rarely covered is that the Gross Domestic Product since 1967 has quadrupled. The average share of wealth for Americans is $12.5 trillion, $41,579 per capita compared to $3.8 trillion, $18,951 per capita in 1967.

While the income and wealth may not be evenly distributed, many have created massive amounts of wealth, more than any other time in history. This is why we have more entrepreneurs than ever; we have more money and opportunity than ever to go after.

I worked with an associate who said, "If you want to get fat on you, hang around a lard barrel." If you want to get rich, live in a rich country. If you think like an entrepreneur, you will see this is the best time in history to get rich.

If you bought a home years ago, and you live in a major metropolitan area, it is likely inflation has at least partially kept you up with inflation. Millions of homeowners have had a financial windfall of spectacular home price increases while the cost of mortgage money has gone down.

The result is millions of people grew richer by borrowing money against the equity in their homes and refinanced mortgages as rates went lower. Many were able to put tens of thousands of tax-free dollars in their pockets and wind up with a lower mortgage payment after refinancing. The cost of currency and money went down; the value of real assets literally went through the roof.

How well you have done financially in the late twentieth century may have a lot more to do with a good inflation investment than with what you earned.

A 10 House Career

Many financial advisors claim a home is not an investment because you live in it. They say a home only becomes an investment when it is sold. However, anyone who has seen their $50,000 dollar tract home inflate to over one million dollars will be thinking something else.

From the 1970's through 2000, I followed a career in broadcasting. We had a growing family and every time we moved to an opportunity, we bought a home. During my career, we bought 10 homes and lived in Flanders NJ, Miami FL, Bel Air MD, Towson MD, Orlando FL, Kahala-Diamond Head HI, Potomac MD, New Canaan CT, La Jolla CA, and Phoenix AZ.

We took the price of the homes we bought and with the help of http://www.zillow.com, we were able to estimate how much the homes would be worth in 2006. We paid $1,810,000 for those homes over time and in 2006, they are worth approximately $8,786,329.

Calculating the inflation of the U.S. dollar over those years, you would find $300,000 dollars in 1970 would be worth $1,558,762 in 2006. Also, if you were to buy exactly the same products in 2006 and 1970, they would cost you $300,000 and $56,480 respectively. To calculate inflation, go the U.S. Department of Labor Bureau of Labor Statistics CPI inflation calculator at http://data.bls.gov/cgi-bin/cpicalc.pl

The following table shows the steady march upward of inflation. If you owned a home during this period your home at least partially kept you even. However, average workers incomes did not keep up. What one income earner was able to provide during the 1970's and 1980's now takes two incomes.

Inflation shrinks the middle class and the value of the dollar. The rich get richer because they own assets and real estate that benefit from inflation.

U.S. Retail Price Inflation 1970-2006:

1970 = 5.7%   1971 = 4.4%   1972 = 3.2%   1973 = 6.2%
1974 = 11.0% 1975 = 9.1%   1976 = 5.8%   1977 = 6.5%
1978 = 7.6%   1979 = 11.3% 1980 = 13.5% 1981 = 10.3%
1982 = 6.2%   1983 = 3.2%   1984 = 4.3%   1985 = 3.60%
1986 = 1.9%   1987 = 3.60% 1988 = 4.1%   1989 = 4.8%
1990 = 5.4%   1991 = 4.2%   1992 = 3.0%   1993 = 3.0%
1994 = 2.6%   1995 = 2.8%   1996 = 3.0%   1997 = 2.3%
1998 = 1.6%   1999 = 2.2%   2000 = 3.40% 2001 = 2.8%
2002 = 1.6%   2003 = 2.3%   2004 = 2.68% 2005 = 3.40%
2006 = 3.2%

A home *is* the lifetime investment for many and as you can see from the table above, and my example of buying homes, real estate has been the lifesaver for most families. Those who rented a home without an inflation hedge were left far behind.

You can get money out of your home in equity and now that investment is paying you in tax-free dollars! The equity that the average American has been able to get out of their homes is what has kept the economy flying at the end of the 20th Century. Trillions of tax-free dollars dumped into the hands of consumers during the 1995-2005 periods as home prices went higher and the cost of borrowing went to the lowest level in 50 years.

Being a homeowner, you may be financially better off today that any time in your life. The average household net worth in 2006 is $465,000 up 83% from 1965 and up

35% from 1995. If you were to take out home ownership equity, these numbers would fall by almost one half.

The rich and wealthy are getting richer and wealthier; they are not following the news for the average working American who continues to fall further and further behind.

The government favors people in business over earned income taxpayers or wage earners. If you own a business, you have opportunities to control your taxes. As a wage earner, you have few options but to pay more and more of your income in higher and higher tax brackets.

The More You Earn, The More You Pay

Taxes can take the single largest bite out of your budget although most people do not consider taxes a budget item. While working for wages, *how much you actually earn is deceptive*. It's what you get to keep *after taxes* that matters. When you earn W-2 wages, you pay the full income tax determined by your tax bracket. The more you earn, the larger percentage of your income goes to taxes.

Once your income hits a certain threshold, the AMT (alternative minimum tax) kicks in and you begin to lose the important major deductions of lower tax brackets. A joint income can easily push wage earners into AMT territory.

To calculate what you are really paying in taxes, add FICA, Medicare and state taxes to the federal tax. When you total everything, you may find your real tax bill approaching 50% of your gross income.

Government Favors Assets Over Wages

The taxes you pay on capital gains are set at dramatically lower percentage, and in many cases, less than half of the percentage that comes out of a payroll check. When you buy and sell something and qualify for the capital gains tax rate, you pay at the lower tax rate regardless of how much income you make.

One of the important reasons people trade and hold real estate is the extraordinary favorable tax advantages. Real estate transactions are able to avoid taxes by trading a "Like Kind" exchange. You roll your capital gains tax forward and pay it later, if at all. Like the advantages many business owners enjoy, real estate has some of the best long-term tax avoidance and advantages in our tax system.

> **The Government Is Telling You: Buy A Business And Buy Real Estate And We Will Do Everything We Can To Make It Worth Your While.**

A job in the last generation was an opportunity to create wealth, if not get rich. It was relatively easy to get wealthy over a lifetime of work. Today that is virtually impossible.

If you want to get rich and wealthy and retire early in the 21st century, think your way through the maze of changes to our workplace, economy, and the global competition. Take advantage of changes and use them as opportunities.

Playing By the Rules of the Rich

Rule #1. Creating Wealth Is A Way Of Thinking.

If you think you can get wealthy, you can get wealthy. Creating wealth demands that you become financially literate. Do not waste your time trying to change things you have no control over.

People writing newspaper and financial articles may have little real world financial experience, yet they are advising with lightweight advice. Get your information from proven professionals. Get advice how to buy real estate from an investor who is successfully doing real estate deals, not a real estate sales person trying to sell you something. Get your financial information from wealthy people, not people who talk wealth but have not been able to create it for themselves. Information is free but information is not knowledge.

Life is short, time is money. Do not run around in circles trying to reinvent the wheel. All you have to do is stop and think. If you are not following what the rich do, you are going to have a hard time getting rich. Learn from professionals and from the accomplished and do not follow the crowd or you will end up average. The crowd is average and all they do is talk. Many are negative because they cannot figure out how to create wealth. If you want to get rich, think like the rich and play by the rules of the rich.

Rule #2. Tax Rules are Skewed to the Rich

Getting rich is a game. The people who take the risks get the rewards. If you work for a paycheck and are a W-2 employee, you are in the worst of all worlds. The more you make, the less you keep of what you earn. As your income passes $65,000, you may find yourself double taxed with AMT or the Alternative Minimum Tax.

W-2 employees have taxes taken out of their paychecks. They have very few options, if any.

Business owners, entrepreneurs, and the rich pay less tax because they create economic development and they employ people. For helping make the economy grow and creating jobs, they are rewarded with tax advantages and incentives. People in business have the ability to control their taxes and legally do the best for themselves, their investments, and their businesses.

The rich get richer not only because they make more money, *they earn a lot of money without paying much, if any, in taxes.* The capital gains tax is a big winner for the rich and much less tax than a W-2 earner pays. The rich and business people have the tax advantage of being able to depreciate and amortize property and investments, while wage earners just pay more and more as their incomes go higher.

Rule #3. Make Inflation Work for You

Plan to live with inflation. Make it work for you, not against you. If you do not pay attention to the long-term effect of inflation, it may be virtually impossible to create wealth. As part of your investments, you should use the leverage of OPM. (OPM or *Other People's Money* is Wall Street slang using borrowed funds by individuals or companies to increase the return on invested capital.) Borrow money to make money and do as the rich and business people do.

Acquire hard assets and real estate as a long-term inflation hedge. While anything can happen, the smart bet is as the population grows, more and more people will be chasing ever-decreasing real estate. They do not make more land. Everyone needs to live somewhere.

Real estate prices, over time, are part of the foundation to creating wealth. Do your homework and not just look at the short-term and flipping properties; real wealth is created in the long-term. The safest way to invest in real estate is to understand numbers and look at real estate as a long-term inflation hedge. It is a fact that, if you are able to hold on long enough, few investments, if any, have the tax advantages or the year-over-year gains of real estate. You should get professional help and learn as much as you can but you should have a portion of your assets protected against inflation with real property.

Rule #4. Think Like and Be an Entrepreneur

The number one asset for generating cash flow and getting rich: owning your own business. The role the government plays in the wealth game is it rewards business owners and investors with benefits and lower taxes while penalizing income earners and those on salaries. The government rewards those who are willing to take the risk by adjusting the tax advantages. A business you own will give you long-term control of your income. You will not be fired or downsized from your own company; all you have to do is keep it profitable.

A business may be held for years or it can be sold and new ones formed. Business is a hedge against inflation and you control the hedge. Rewards for the entrepreneur look better and better as more money

circulates. You can get rich younger and faster because
the opportunity to get rich is greater. In order for the
government to combat competitive forces and fight
inflation, it is printing money faster than we can spend
it. The cash liquidity in the economy is like fishing in
the ocean compared to a pond of years ago.

We no longer count millionaires as super rich. We
count the billionaires as the new financially successful.
In the 1960's we thought Joe Namath was doing well
earning $142,000 ($848,000 in 2007 dollars). In 2007,
Tiger Woods approaches $100,000,000.

CEO's of large corporations used to earn 40 times the
average income of workers. Today they earn over 400
times the average worker; executive income is counted
in the tens of millions of dollars.

Rule #5. Put Your Money to Work
Assets will feed you. Liabilities will eat you. Invest
wisely and be a smart money manager. Learn how to
spend money. Start with savings and invest as you
earn more. Learn more; get financial intelligence.
Education and knowledge alone will not make you rich
but when you apply intelligence to money, you have no
limits. Be proactive and make things happen or your
knowledge and education will be useless. Money will
not make money by itself. The goal is to be in the same
position as the wealthy. The rich have money working
for them, the poor and middle class are going to work
for money.

The more money you have working for you, the faster you get to your goals. Compound interest multiplies money and creates riches. Hustle while you are young. The earlier you start investing, the better you finish.

Rule #6. Use OPM to Create Wealth

Use debt as leverage. It is virtually impossible to get rich on your own resources; you need the help of others. Unless you have rich parents to help or you won the lottery, it will take years to get what you can accomplish by thinking and taking smart actions. People who are rich and wealthy are looking to invest money and put it to work. They are happy to get a fair return on investments. The important business principle of using money to make money in personal planning creates wealth. Do not use debt to buy luxuries and things that depreciate until you are far ahead of the game. You create your future by what you do today so you cannot start soon enough. Get the best advice you can from tax advisors and successful investment professionals.

Men and Women Out-Think Men or Women

Women possess instincts that make them as good, if not better than men at investing. Men tend to be more assertive and aggressive but those natural instincts may not create wealth as much as a women's long-term instinct to hold and build. The balance of men and women working together is far better than a team of men or a team of women by themselves. Creating wealth is a team sport; it is a game of chess, not checkers. Creating wealth takes time, thinking, and strategy. When you look for partners and people to help you in your thinking, planning and doing, be sure you have capable men and women on the team.

Education Is Your Key to Getting Rich and Wealthy

Getting rich is a way of thinking. Your behavior and your habits come from your thinking. The financially literate are the people most likely to get rich and even more likely to hold on to it. People in business get rich because they take the risk. Entrepreneurs, investors, and business people have the ability to make unlimited money and the government is playing favorites supporting them over W-2 workers and paycheck earners. Think for yourself and get the best advice you can afford. Getting rich is a mind game, be sure your mind is in good working order.

> **If It Were Easy To Get Rich, The People Advising You Would Not Be Telling You How To Do It. They Would Be Doing It Themselves.**

Rich and Free
Entrepreneur's Guide

- Understand the power and force of compound interest.
- Protecting yourself against Inflation.
- Manage cash flow.
- Spending money is as important as making money.
- The rich have money working for them, the poor work for money.
- Use OPM to make more money.
- Buy assets that will take care of you.
- Don't accumulate liabilities that will eat you.

Chapter 11

Why the Rich Get Richer and the Poor Get Squeezed

Our economy looks like a circle with two sides being gently compressed by a ThighMaster.

—unknown

The successful have it and they are living it up. They buy exotic cars costing hundreds of thousands of dollars and cruise on large mega yachts that look like floating mansions. They build trophy homes as big as libraries and create home movie theaters costing millions of dollars. Some of their indoor sports courts are bigger than your high school gym. They pay fabulous sums for luxuries cooked up just for them. The mega-rich have exorbitant wealth, more than any time in history.

According to the 2007 Forbes Magazine billionaire study, of the world's 946 billionaires, 415 are U.S. citizens. Germany has 55, Russia 53, India 36, United Kingdom 29,

Turkey 25, Japan 24 and on down the line. Fifty-three nations in total have billionaire citizens.

To put a fifteen billion dollar fortune in perspective, it is a pile of money approximately 60 feet high, 150 feet long, and 62½ feet deep. Fifteen billion dollar bills laid end to end would circle the globe at the equator 60 times.

The distribution of wealth worldwide is far from equal and the disparity is the same for the richest country in the world. The average and middle class is shrinking while the rich are getting richer. Real wages are flat and have been for years. The cost of college has put millions of people in debt. Tens of millions cannot afford the cost of health insurance. Young couples are not having kids because they need dual incomes for survival.

The average and middle class are in paycheck paralysis yet the U.S. is the best country in which to create wealth. The U.S. encourages free enterprise and grants favors and tax advantages to business, corporations, and special interest groups. The system works for those willing to take a risk and hustle.

The Squeeze

You cannot accumulate wealth if you spend more than you take in. The long-term affect of inflation is when wages stay flat and even, it squeezes the average and middle class. With inflation, it's critical that you continue to move ahead. If you stand still, inflation will make you poorer and poorer.

My father warned me about inflation.

"I'm going to tell you a secret," he said.

"You will never achieve real success if you just worry about expenses. The answer is to make more money. You will never be able to control what things will cost. You get ahead by outrunning inflation. Things will work for you if you keep making more money every year. Don't get behind," he warned.

Unfortunately, even for those who have been hustling, many have not been able to outrun inflation.

The problem for the young and the poor is they are on the wrong side of inflation. They do not have ownership of resources and assets that appreciate.

What has helped many is homeownership. Real estate has been riding the inflation wave for years. Paying off a mortgage creates equity and with rising home prices, it creates a piggy bank for the homeowner.

For those starting out, it is a hard time to be young. Higher home prices force many to borrow more than reasonable and they struggle with mortgages out of proportion to incomes. The hope for a new and first time homeowner is to earn more income in the future to cover the debt. A high mortgage payment that needs two average incomes limits lifestyle and the ability to make other investments. People become house poor yet real estate rich.

You See It After It Happens

Trying to spot inflation is like trying to watch grass grow. You can watch the grass, but you will not see it grow. When you come back a week later, you see the growth. Inflation grows like grass, it silently moves higher and higher. It's over time you see the dramatic changes in price and value.

As the dollar buys less and inflation moves higher, families need two incomes to survive. The average income has not kept up with inflation and is barely enough to support one person.

In the past generation, the average family of four lived on one income. Most moms stayed home to raise the kids and run the household.

Who is to Blame?

We can blame companies for being greedy and blame politicians for favoring special interests. We can blame inflation or we can blame our education system for not preparing us to deal with the new economy. However, it's a bigger picture that's shaping the future.

U.S. workers earn higher salaries than most of the world. In the past, most countries could not compete with the U.S. because of the lead in technology and ingenuity. However, just as technology and communications gave the U.S. a decided advantage, those advantages have become available worldwide.

As countries grow, the U.S. has lost much of its manufacturing base not because of products, but because of the higher cost of doing business.

Companies that have the advantage of lower labor costs are able to increase their share of business. Most of the U.S. jobs lost are not gone; they are alive in foreign lands. Other companies in foreign countries are selling stuff we used to make back to us, at lower prices.

Competition has lowered the cost of goods. Worldwide manufacturing and competition is telling us we will continue to see a shift and re-distribution of wealth in the future. Inflation, competition, and flat salaries have the American middle class under attack.

Yet even with the problems of competition, the U.S. has a strong economy. While many high paying jobs are gone, unemployment remains low. Innovation and opportunity continue to create jobs. The U.S. middle class is a lower class after the haircut of global competition. However, the economy grows and moves ahead.

The U.S. does not have to win the economic race by itself. More than one country can have prosperity and good economic times. However, the U.S. must remain competitive and a frontrunner in order to keep up the standard of living.

The problem is how wealth is distributed and how can *you* get in on worldwide prosperity. Most of us would rather see a more even distribution of wages, income, and opportunity but that is a society and political issue and more than any one of us can deal with.

Deal with forces under your control, not out of your influence. Deal with the cards you are dealt, not with what you consider ideal.

The Last Time This Happened

The 21st century began with a generational change. It's similar to the end of the agricultural age where farmers were the big employers.

Farmers instantly became more productive with new technology as tractors and machinery changed everything. Farms needed fewer workers to tend the field, productivity went up, and costs went down. Technology brought the end to an agricultural era and a new age of industrialization began. Work moved to the cities and so did workers as new industries created jobs.

As we move further in the age of information and knowledge, social and economic transformation creates winners and losers just as it has in past generational change. Not only is new knowledge and information being produced, the old knowledge is being reinterpreted and repackaged. Competition is between the slow and the fast, there is a constant need to learn new skills to remain competitive.

The "New Economy" was a term coined in the early 1990's. Looking back, we can see changes to the new economy were just starting; the big social and economic events are ahead.

Wealth creation happens fast today because we have more people with more money and an increasing market in world trade. A good idea can generate an avalanche of business and make money faster than ever. Companies go from start-up to billions in record time.

The Law of Supply and Demand

Productivity has caused lower wages for the middle class, **but it has also created immense wealth in the economy!** The new wealth tools are financial literacy, independent thinking, and an entrepreneurial spirit.

In our "global" economy, distinctions between domestic and foreign worker no longer matter as much. In foreign nations and foreign corporations, workers are competing in the same global marketplace as their American counterparts. Other countries use the same technologies and strategies in business.

The worldwide market is setting wages. These forces make it more difficult to manage companies. However, technology and productivity keep mid-level and salaried workers at a competitive disadvantage. Top executives that can successfully run a company in global competition earn even higher wages.

The spread between worker and executive income widens. It is the law of supply and demand. Top-notch CEO and executive talent is hard to find while we have an oversupply of workers and managers.

Follow the Money

As inflation grows, the dollar loses value and the government prints more money. How to take advantage and profit from the massive amounts of money and liquidity in the marketplace is the question.

While it's not a good time to be an average worker, it's a spectacular time to be an entrepreneur. Technology allows anyone to compete in the worldwide market. If you can compete across states lines, you can compete across countries.

Technology, communications, the internet, and free world wide markets have changed the economy. Entrepreneurial opportunities are at an all time high while the workplace is over crowded with bright people holding college degrees. Good jobs that pay well are limited and in huge demand, while many average income jobs are readily available.

Look outside of the traditional way of earning a living, because the *rules have changed*. The problem for the average worker has become an opportunity for independent thinkers and entrepreneurs.

New thinking may not be as risky as you think. It may be more risk to continue at a dead end job or one that may be eliminated because of productivity and competition.

Unless you are one of the top executives earning a higher income, it may be time to re-think the game. There is a sea of money out there, but you may be drowning in old ways of thinking. Think beyond an old education and last generation's paradigms.

People will survive but their lifestyles will suffer if they do not take advantage of the opportunities change brings. Either you are moving with the times or you risk being run over by them.

The key is to become more enterprising and think like an entrepreneur. Learn new skills and don't waste time on things you did not create or things you cannot control.

Rich and Free Entrepreneur's Guide

- The rich get richer because they are on the winning side of inflation.
- Inflation is a treadmill: earn more or you will fall off.
- More money in the hands of people makes good ideas happen faster.
- Follow the money; look for new opportunities in change.
- Think global, technology allows bigger opportunities.

Chapter 12

Overschooled and Undereducated?

He was so learned that he could name a horse in nine languages; so ignorant that he bought a cow to ride on.
—**Benjamin Franklin**

The Fifties was the Golden Age of Television. Variety shows and westerns dominated the screen while sports figures and athletes were coming of age as millions watched live action sports. Professional athletes became sensations and Mark McCormack saw opportunity in the power of television. In 1960, Mark signed his first client, world famous golfer Arnold Palmer. The sports marketing industry and athlete representation was about to be revolutionized.

Mark signed superstars Tiger Woods, Pete Sampras, Charles Barkley and others. He created new business opportunities with endorsements, merchandising and sports programming for television. Mark became one of the most powerful men in sports, and the world's first super-agent. He founded IMG, International Management Group, a worldwide sports and entertainment company. Revenues grew into billions of dollars.

Mark was a graduate of Yale Law School and a guest lecturer at the Harvard Business School. While teaching, he discovered bright students were asking naïve questions. Mark realized lessons that he had learned were not taught in business school. That led him to writing the best seller, *What They Don't Teach You at Harvard Business School: Notes From A Street-Smart Executive.*

Mark was thumbing his nose at formal education in a sense but not so much to criticize Harvard as to compliment education with "street smarts." In 1985, Mark said in an audio session from a *Street Smart Executive:*

> *In fairness to the Harvard Business School, what they don't teach you is what they can't teach you. My main purpose in recording this program is to fill in many of the gaps --- the gaps between a business school education and the street knowledge that comes from the day-to-day experience of running a business and managing people.*

Mark was an entrepreneur, salesman, negotiator, and a master at marketing. He also had the ability to "read" people. His people skills led him to unique insight and negotiating skills. He understood what motivated people. Mark was a relentless worker. He made mistakes but he didn't let that bother him. Everything was a learning experience to do better next time.

Where Does Our Thinking Come From?

When I was in school, I was smart enough to know the education system was designed to reward a good memory and weed out the less intelligent or "dumb" people. The system, from grade school on, rewarded students with good memories.

Teaching obedient behavior with fear of failing is one form of motivating kids. It does not breed independent thinking, creativity and imagination and it's sure not fun and exciting. Once past elementary school, many students realize the system is as much a babysitting service and social playground as it is about education.

Games, simulations, and real-life experience are the best teachers. People learn by doing. Education is a self-directed activity; you cannot pour knowledge and smarts into someone. How much you learn is dependent on the *desire to learn*.

In the classroom, memory is easy to test. However, the right brain skills of creativity and innovation only require average memory yet those skills are the hardest to test. It's difficult to teach right brain skills in a structured environment. The real world does not look or act anything like a classroom.

> *The only thing that interferes with my learning is my education.*
> **—Albert Einstein**

Schools teach math in a complex manner instead of the real math used in jobs and careers. Educators see the limitations of the system and they are working to improve it. However, many graduate with few skills to help them in the real world.

Obsolete high schools graduate uninspired kids who go on to college with little more ambition than just to be able to get a job. They take courses with little real life value and study what appeals to them as long as they get a degree. Students who give it little thought end up with an education that leads to an average income.

We educate with strategies of a past generation and prepare students for jobs. We should also be preparing students not to have a job and teach them how to be entrepreneurs and create their own livelihoods. Many go through college doing what they want to do but the money may not follow.

To become wealthy, learn skills that will make you money. You may have to force yourself to take courses and learn things that you would otherwise avoid. It's one thing to figure out how to hold a job but it's something else figuring out how to get rich. It takes experience and knowledge to create wealth. People smart enough to graduate college are capable, but without financial literacy and the right skills, they may be able to do little beyond hold a job.

Sheepwalking a Job

Seth Godin, author and marketing guru, sees companies taking advantage of the education system. Companies hire "Sheepwalkers," people who have been raised to be obedient. Many companies give people braindead jobs and use fear to keep them in line.

> Training a student to be sheepish is a lot easier than the alternative. Teaching to the test, ensuring compliant behavior and using fear as a motivator are the easiest and fastest ways to get a kid through school. So why does it surprise us that we graduate so many sheep?

Hiring sheepwalkers is a way to keep salaries in line. People come out of school and college and fall back on what they have been taught. They may be well educated but nevertheless, compliant.

You are your information. You are what you think.

What you learn is what you become; you are your experience. You may be trained with industrial age education but that does not mean you have to *be* an industrial age thinker. You may be computer literate and technically savvy, but how you think may be a bigger handicap than you realize. Education and a higher degree will help you get a better job but it's no guarantee you will be successful at the job or make good income.

The combination of a formal education and "street smarts" is what makes you successful. You can be taught leadership skills and entrepreneurial theory but that does not mean you come out of a classroom a leader or entrepreneur. Moreover, you cannot give people tenacity while that is easy enough to explain in a classroom.

Why Is It So Hard to Unlearn?

Our rose-colored glasses and paradigms prevent us from seeing new ideas. If your education has made you literate but unable to think how you can get rich and wealthy, it may be because the training and environment was job oriented and compliant. Become an independent thinker and think for yourself.

Paradigms can blind you to creative ideas and solutions. This phenomenon called the "Paradigm Effect" means you can be too close to things to see them. The invention of the quartz electric watch is a classic paradigm story.

For centuries, the Swiss were excellent watchmakers. Few could match the beauty and quality of their handmade creations and thousands worked in the profession. Around 1960, the Swiss invented an electronic watch, a quartz timepiece. It was accurate but of no use to anyone. It had no gears, precious stones, and hand-made details. The Swiss thinking was who would want such a simple watch?

Visiting executives from Japan were in Switzerland and shown this new invention. They saw something different than the Swiss were seeing. Different cultures and people can have different visions and mindsets. As this quartz watch had no perceived value to the Swiss, the Japanese were able to buy the rights for a small price.

It did not take long for the Japanese to figure out how to make accurate watches for very little money. They brought excellent timepieces to the marketplace for fraction of the cost of Swiss watches. Japanese manufacturers gained an edge in the watch industry and the Swiss watchmakers lost the leadership and thousands of jobs. A new market was created and an old market was re-positioned. More people could now afford an accurate watch and a new disruptive technology changed the industry overnight. The Swiss were blinded by success.

> **You Cannot Challenge an Assumption You Do Not Know You Have Made.**

The paradigms of ritual, and the obedience of your education, may prevent you from seeing things differently. Life writes new rules, it's your job to stay alert and see old things in new ways as well as look for new opportunities.

Age will become a liability if you let it. As we gain knowledge and information, even ten years out of college may be enough to leave you behind. While the young may have less experience, they have current education and knowledge. Their information is not out of date. It's street smarts *and* education that create success. In the information age, keep your information current.

Focus On What Works

I worked for entrepreneurs and learned new skills. As my income was based on commissions, I had to become a quick study. If I were to survive, it would be on my creativity, innovation, and resources. I was given the tools to make a living, but how much of a living was up to me.

I not only learned how to manage companies but I was trained to be an entrepreneur. In order for my boss to be sure I focused on the important things, I was given equity and became vested in the company. The real financial rewards were going to come to me only when the company was sold. My salary in the beginning was average, but my potential was huge.

I learned that politics in an entrepreneurial business would only waste time. Winning would be the ability to create something better and capitalize on opportunities. My job was not to come to work, it was to make things happen.

I was a contract entrepreneur and hired for services. As soon as that service ended, I would be out of a job. I would be unemployed but richer.

Coming from a background in sales helped my success. I took on more responsibility and learned new skills. I had good mentors but I did not think of them as bosses, even though they were. My independent thinking and drive helped my success; the company gave me the tools.

My business education came from real-life hands-on experience. I learned how to grow companies and create success. However, when I spent time with managers from other companies, I could see that my goals and thinking were different. Managers without equity were doing a job and they focused on keeping that job.

I focused on operating success and opportunity. I would earn no equity with average safe performance; I had to take calculated risks or I would never reach my goals. At that point, I realized I was not going to be happy doing anything unless I had a stake in it.

Like Father, Like Son

My son was 26 years old working for a large Japanese rechargeable battery manufacturer in California. The management team wanted to be sure his department was aligned with company policy. They brought in a consultant experienced in sales and motivation. The consultant studied the company and called a sales meeting.

The tone of the meeting was positive but it was a sophomoric atmosphere. The sales team setting was like a high school classroom and the consultant was an energetic teacher with little other than classroom experience.

The questions began. Everyone was to share with the group how sales were doing. The follow up question was everyone had to explain his or her personal goals. Answers went around the conference table.

The sales people answered the questions in a reserved manner. Many of the sales people disagreed with company policies but were not about to get into confrontation with a consultant.

When it came to sharing personal goals, you could sense the answers were made up on the spot. Goals ranged from paying off the car to long-term plans of buying a condominium.

My son answered his goal was to create $6,000 a month passive income after taxes.

That answer stopped the meeting. It got everyone's attention. During the recess, the sales people asked my son why he said his goal was for passive income. They did not understand how that could be done. Did he really mean income coming in without working? How would he do that? Would he still have to have a job?

My son was surprised not one person on the sales team ever thought of the idea of working towards passive income.

When I heard the story, I roared but I was not surprised. I told my son that the answer he gave was too entrepreneurial to share in a corporate environment.

The sales people felt the meeting was corporate positioning and not really designed to help the sales effort. So the sales people were not willing to give honest answers. My son did give an honest answer and it was the best one in the meeting. However, it was not the answer anyone expected. It's all in how you think.

> **What Most People Want Is Freedom But They Go After Survival.**

An entrepreneur is proactive. The price for being free is the risk you are willing to take. Everything is a risk; nothing in life is a guarantee. All risk is relative. A "safe job" is an oxymoron and there is no such thing. You never own a job. A job is the time you are willing to give that someone else is willing to pay for. In spite of your value, any job can end.

However, a business or venture you control is yours. All you have to do is keep it profitable and moving forward. The challenge in your thinking will be letting go of dependence on job thinking. The hard part of being an entrepreneur is you cannot shift the responsibility. There is nowhere to pass it.

You leverage knowledge and skills. If your education is leading you to what you enjoy but not making you wealthy, you have to make a decision. If you want to get rich, do what the rich do and focus on wealth creating skills.

That may lead you to do things you would rather not be doing. You can do whatever you want with your time. However, how you spend your time may have little relationship to creating wealth and getting rich.

Being poor and staying poor are two different things. Anyone can make a mistake and lose money. Anyone can be raised in a poor environment.

To be poor is one thing. To stay poor is a choice. You are limited only by your skills and specialized education. You may have a good education but that means little if it won't get you to your goals.

You have to decide what you want to do. If you work at a job, it will not make you rich. *It's what you do while you're not working that will make your wealth.* If you become an entrepreneur, you take more risk but you have unlimited upside potential. The Way To Create Wealth And Riches Is To Do The Following:

1. Own Your Own Business And Continue To Grow And Operate The Business Profitably.

2. Invest Your Money Wisely And Create Passive Income That Will Support You Without You Working.

A job gives you immediate income and hopefully enough money extra for other things. *A job will also buy you time to think how to get out of your job.* A job pays the bills. However, your future and riches are created by what you do at night, on weekends and days off. The time you are not on the job belongs to you. That is the time to work and plan the future.

Your future is created by what you do today, not tomorrow.

—Robert Kiyosaki

The research and education you gain thinking and working on your own behalf is your entrepreneurial side. Even while you work for others, be thinking like an entrepreneur.

A company creates a future by growing and improving its product and service. A company or business looks for new opportunities and new markets.

Think of yourself as the CEO of your own enterprise. Do the same thing for you as a company does for its future. Look for opportunity, learn new skills, and plan your own future.

Going to work and doing a job is not creating a future, it's covering expenses and keeping you in place. As a worker in a company, you are helping others create wealth and riches but those riches are not for you. You do not own the success of your job or company.

> **You Own What You Are Willing To Do For Yourself.**

Classroom learning helps you become literate and knowledgeable but has little to do with creating wealth and getting rich. It is up to you to decide if a job will get you to your goals or simply meet your current needs and expenses.

As more people vie for the fewer good jobs that pay well, the high bar employers use to knock people out of the running is even more education and experience. The more education and experience you have, the better shape you are in to land a better job or move up in your company.

However, you may find yourself highly educated and over schooled for a basic job because that may be all that is available to you. As we have more qualified workers than we have good high-paying jobs, companies continue to raise the high bar even for entry-level jobs. That is why a degree is essential in the working world; it's a ticket to ride.

But the ride may be no better than it was years ago and it may be a much slower ride to good income. Holding a job long term may give you a false sense of security. Jobs most often will not keep pace with inflation. In order to stay even, continually work your way up the ladder but no one says it has to be the company ladder.

The riskiest thing you may be doing is accepting the fact that you are stuck in a job. Riches come from specialized knowledge and education, not general literacy. Being an entrepreneur has little to do with formal degrees. Effort you put into learning the skills to get you rich is the education you need to create wealth.

Rich and Free Entrepreneur's Guide

- What they can't teach you in school is what you must learn.
- You may be up to date with out of date education.
- Don't stop learning.
- Riches may not follow simply because you have a degree or higher education.
- Educate yourself with skills that can make you rich and wealthy.

Chapter 13

Turbulence Ahead: Fasten Seat Belts

Innovation is the specific instrument of entrepreneurship. The act that endows resources with a new capacity to create wealth.

— Peter Drucker

Could everyone please return to your seat and strap yourself in tightly. There is fresh turbulence ahead and the ride could get bumpy. Changes in society and technology are far from stabilizing. We are moving into a period of turbulent times, which will likely lead to significant structural changes over the next 25 years or so.

Radical obsolescence can make products and services essentially useless and worthless overnight. Changes will be necessary for business to remain competitive in tomorrow's marketplace.

Innovations are reshaping everything from health care, medicine, biotech, wireless, nanotech, computers, communication, automobiles, food, and robotics. Things are changing at an ever accelerated rate.

Nanotechnology is one of the emerging sciences that will have a dramatic effect on our future. Nanotechnology is the science of super miniaturization and it will enable us to change the very essence of material and matter smaller than one micrometer. It will create products so small it will change our clothing, food, medicine, and virtually every aspect of our lives. Nanomaterials will become commonplace as this new science advances.

The challenge for business and entrepreneurs in the fast emerging global marketplace will be to figure out who is the customer, what do they need, how can you reach them, and how do you sell to them?

Your success may depend on whether you approach change as an opportunity or a threat. People complain about there being too much change. Things are moving too quickly, and many of the changes are disruptive. Some manage to get through while others grumble and watch.

Threat or Opportunity?

Dramatic change creates opportunities and people who do their homework will get in at the beginning. Powerful companies and societies will fail as they expect past resources and strength to protect them from the forces of change. It won't.

The shift in power away from old guard and elite will be felt in every field. The bigger the company, the harder they fall if they don't remain competitive.

A business protects itself by trying to create a monopoly or keeping its knowledge and information as confidential as possible. Keeping others from figuring out how things are done is standard business practice. But keeping secrets today is a lot harder.

Secrets? What Secrets!

Today, what information is not available? Secrets are available to anyone who is willing to take the time to learn. The internet created an audience that is demanding content and ideas at an insatiable rate. It's a paradigm shift for corporations to learn how to deal with the good and bad news. What used to be confidential is now common information.

Television will continue to dominate our time but its form, content, and means of delivery will change. Consumers will have access to direct and specific content customized on demand. An unlimited supply of entertainment and information will be available, more than anyone has time to view.

Information will become more personalized. Computers in some form will be the brains or hub of our entertainment centers and the internet will become the new audio and video network of communication.

Television was the big step in mass education and communication. It created instant news, information, and communication. Television changed advertising, business, and society. Daily newspaper circulation falls as the younger generation grows older and gets most of their information from faster electronic sources.

The consumer is more and more in control. People will decide their own source of entertainment, information, and education. Consumers will get what they want to see, not simply what networks want to broadcast.

Change is exciting and unsettling. It brings opportunity and it creates challenges. Competition from India and China will challenge Europe and America for power and control of consumer demands. We look forward to a more level playing field and distribution of power. The entrepreneurs will follow the money.

The free flow of information is driving technological revolution. The content of the media is evolving and changing to meet the needs of the contemporary audience worldwide.

Since the beginning of time, technology has driven history. The challenge is to understand *how* change will shape the future of business society. Challenges will remake things as we break them with new way of doing things.

Change is the opportunity while it devastates old inefficient ways of doing things. The faster the consumer figures things out, the faster inefficient companies and businesses fall. Every new technology tackles the old to the ground. It forces the inefficient to get up to speed or get out of the way.

As enlightened consumers get smarter and smarter, companies will be running to keep up with them. People will get rich and wealthy figuring out how to get products and services in the hands of customers. As we move forward, the entire rulebook of what is *supposed to be* will no longer exist. As a new generation comes into power, the older generation must keep up with changes or lose its relevance. You cannot hold on to the past for security and safety.

Success is a way of thinking. Be confident that you are capable of getting your share of wealth. Knowing how to improvise, be action oriented, and think on your feet is a skill and knowledge you acquire from experience.

You need to be a freethinking spirit because you will not have many doing this kind of thinking for you. As the adage goes, if it were easy, they would be doing it themselves.

Don't Fall in Love with Ideas

A successful thinker is flexible. You cannot fall in love or embrace any one idea. However, many do create an original idea and fall in love with it. The problem is, the good idea may not be so hot, and it might be a dud. Without a second or third idea in the wings, many are reluctant to let go of that original single idea. People who put ego in front of brains are people who need to be right. Even when they are wrong! One of the hidden reasons that people fail is their lack of a second or third idea.

You will never know about your idea until you try to make it work. It is more important to have the *willingness and spirit* to try a new way and dare to be different. That is why it's called "creativity and innovation" and not "dumb and stuck." For everything you do, there is another way of doing it. Be willing to change your thinking if you find a batter way to be successful.

A rigid, hierarchical, inflexible company is slow to change and even slower to see opportunity. Smart thinkers capitalize on the arrogance of others that hold on to old ideas that are not efficient or no longer work. The game is to figure out how to do what a company is not willing to do and take advantage of a blind or rigid bureaucracy.

The will to challenge the status quo takes courage and brass. Learn how to think sideways, upside-down, crooked and color the lines outside of the box. And that's why we have so many younger millionaires today than any time in history.

Young and Willing to Try

Younger people have no allegiance or connection to how things were done; they just look for better ways to do them. They have nothing to protect and everything to gain. It's easier to see things when you are dealing with a blank slate. Many can look at the same picture while only a few see a message. It takes a new perspective to see things differently.

You cannot fall in love with your creativity and ideas unless they prove themselves. When things don't work, look for new solutions and new ideas. Your idea may not have filled a need or created a niche.

People look for the easy way out. It's human nature. But it's not a good way to become successful. Creating wealth is not about easy, it's about being smart. It's about your ability to see change and problems as opportunity while others see nothing but the same old thing.

Change, technology, and innovation are the best friends of the thinker and entrepreneur. In times of extreme changes, you have more and bigger opportunities.

> **Winning Is Not About Chance, It's About Choice.**

One idea is hardly a ballgame. You have to decide if you want to be in the baseball business, or to play in a single game. Being an entrepreneur and innovative thinker looking to create wealth is not a single idea; it's a way of thinking.

The future is to be open minded and flexible as things will happen faster and faster. Change will accelerate. The fastest way to get rich will be to think creatively and use innovation as a tool. Communication has opened up the ability to be in business on a global basis, do not limit your thinking!

Rich and Free Entrepreneur's Guide

- Things are changing exponentially.
- The internet and communication drive change.
- Innovation and creativity demand flexible thinking.
- Being an entrepreneur is not a single idea, it's a way of thinking.
- You don't have to be young, but you need young thinking.

Part 4

Alternative Strategies

Some people have great jobs and they love what they do. They are successful and do not have the desire to create a new career or be on their own.

However, a job still leaves you with a long-term problem. A company will not help you retire and you will not get rich while you work for others.

While working for others, the steps to wealth and riches are in your hands. Making millions and retiring in style will take planning and action.

Chapter 14

Why Only One Source of Income?

Never be afraid to try something new. Remember, amateurs built the Ark, professionals built the Titanic.
—unknown

Many assume entrepreneurs are risk takers. That is a misunderstanding. One of the richest multi-billionaire entrepreneurs and business geniuses of all time describes risk this way.

Risk comes from not knowing what you're doing.
—Warren Buffett

People put time, money, and resources at risk for personal gains. However, making a highly calculated risk with experience, knowledge, and information may be little risk at all.

Entrepreneurs seek personal gain and they organize resources necessary to take advantage of opportunities. So what is the opposite of an entrepreneur? An employee, someone hired as a wage earner.

It is when you stop thinking like an employee you open the door to entrepreneurial thinking. You become more innovative and creative; you open your mind to creating wealth and reaching personal goals.

One Source of Income? Why Only One?

This brings up a concept that flies in the face of conventional thinking. Most people think one source of income is what you should have at a time. That mindset is old thinking from a different era and it is not going to get you closer to freedom and independence.

> **Where is it written in stone,**
> ***"Thou Shalt Only Have***
> ***One Source of Income"***

Do you think making money or starting something new on your time is being unfaithful to your job or company? Is guilt whispering in your ear, "That's not allowed!"

Well, that thinking is what they call indentured servitude and *unfree* labor. Yet the people who do that to themselves are stuck in old paradigms. Many grew up in a generation that lived well on one income, a pension, savings, and social security. In addition, when the house was paid off things looked good.

However, most of our parents did not face the problems and cost of spiraling inflation and stagnant salaries or they would never have achieved so much. Times are different and things are different. Today it takes two jobs in a household to make ends meet and for most, two income are barely adequate.

A Job Is Not Who You Are

A job does not belong to you. It's a position you fill for a period of time, it's a way to earn income. Working for others, *you never give up your unique individual values or identity*. What you do for a living is not what, or who, you are. If your job no longer exists, you are no less a person or individual. You move on to the next opportunity. Your identity belongs to you and that goes wherever you go.

What you do on your own time belongs to you. Who says you cannot be an entrepreneur or do something for yourself while you work for others? Is it fear of failure or an old paradigm that you should devote all of your time to a job or company? Are you really being disloyal or cheating?

This closed-end thinking is exactly the opposite of what your job or company is doing. Companies are on the prowl for opportunities. They pioneer new ideas and ventures or buy out other companies to grow the business. New divisions are added all the time, and why not? Companies have infrastructure in place and workers to help them. So why not make more with the resources they have? That is an important way to expand and grow.

Should you be stuck in time and stand still while a company you work for grows and becomes more profitable?

There is only one success...to be able to spend your life in your own way, and not to give others absurd maddening claims upon it.

—Christopher Morley

In the past, companies promised you that if you put in years of service, you would be able to retire with a pension and medical benefits. In effect, you were offered a form of ownership or equity. You were participating in the success of the company.

So what has happened? In today's competitive business environment, you are a disposable part of the business and not an integral part of an organization. Long-term prospects are only as good as you are a current asset to a company. Companies that do not need your help will end your employment.

That is why you can't afford to be paranoid about your outside ventures unless you have an agreement with your company that says otherwise:

- **First, it is none of their business what you do on your own time.**

- **Second, where in the heck is your future going to come from if you know your job at some point will no longer exist and your income will end?**

You could be unemployed at any point because of being downsized, upsized, outsourced or simply eliminated. A job is a temporary convenience for both you and your employer; it fills an important need at the time. However, do not lose track of where you are in time!

Here is a secret many discover after years of working for others. It is a principle entrepreneurs learn early on.

> **Day Job Thinking Is 9 To 5.**
> **Entrepreneurs Make Things Happen 24/7**

When was the last time you saw a big airplane lumbering down the runway taking it easy and kind of coasting just before take off? Last time I checked, the way to get an airplane off the ground is to gun the engines to max power and go like a bat out of hell. Airplanes only get off the ground if they get up enough speed!

A successful person always finds the time to do more. The more successful they are, the more they seem to be able to do. Low achievers complain, "I'm so busy I'm out of control. I can't do any more!"

That thinking separates the winners and the learners. Find the time to think how you are going to help yourself and create your future because no one else will do it for you. If you do not create time for yourself, wealth, riches and freedom will not fall in your lap.

Hustle While You're Young!

I produced seminars in San Diego for Robert Kiyosaki and the Excellerated Business Schools. One of the best workshops we produced was about creating wealth. It was fast and fun and we played games to teach lessons. People learned more about themselves from their own behavior playing games than we could ever teach them on paper or talking about it. The best lessons are the ones we get from experience.

One of the games we played was to put everyone in a circle around their chairs. We tied their hands together and tied their ankles together. We tied a short rope in-between their hands and ankles so they had to bend over. No one could stand up straight. They could only take baby steps. The game was similar to musical chairs. Everyone had to hustle as best they could around the chairs to the music.

When the music stopped, everyone had to find a seat, but one chair was always missing. Someone was left standing.

The lesson, however, was not to find a place to sit. It was to stress a point that when you are young, you have energy and physical drive. When you have youth and energy that is the time to hustle.

The players in the game caught on quickly: Running around with your legs tied together and stooped over like an old person not only slows you down, you run out of energy in a hurry.

Is it time to become organized when you are old and out of energy? Will you ever have more energy in the future than you do at this very moment?

If you are finished with your formal education, get the lead out, get moving, and don't put things off. If you want to create freedom and wealth, you simply have to get started. Regardless of the junk you see on late night TV and the sensational business books filled with hype, few people become successful overnight.

> **It Takes Time For Things To Work.**

Give up some TV time and some weekends. Get thinking and get something going. Some of the most successful companies of all time started in garages by young people with ideas of being entrepreneurs. Apple Computer and Hewlett Packard started in humble garages. Thomas Edison liked garages, too.

I'm Partial to Dining Room Tables

A napkin scribbled with a great idea that you actually start is worth a 200-page business plan that sits in a file.

If you're young and just starting out and live in an apartment, call mom and tell her to get the stuff out of the garage, you're commandeering the space. Otherwise, I'm partial to dining room and kitchen tables. Whatever works.

This may sound sophomoric. It cannot be this simple to think you can start a new life in a garage or on the dining room table. But yes, that is how many things get started.

Every venture, business, idea, or accomplishment has to start somewhere. If you have been working for 5, 10, 15, or 20 years and you have not tried to do something to help your future but hold a job, what are the odds of you winding up on some beach in the Caribbean with tiny umbrellas in your cocktails?

You may be the one trying to run around the room with your legs tied together taking baby steps and not able to stand up straight.

Everyone who goes out on a limb looks at the ground and thinks, "Holy Cow! I can fall and break a leg. Or worse!" But if you do not take a chance, what is the alternative?

Call Mom or Dad

Get your dad out of retirement and pick his brain or ask mom to help you with her ideas. Whatever you do, do not drudge off to work like a wooden soldier, and pray for the lottery to hit.

Have fun and think of business as a game. Because it is a game! A thinking person's game. One thing I have seen working with rich and successful people is they have fun and they laugh a lot.

Obstacles along the way for the successful are only temporary. They figure out a way to get around them, they don't dwell on them. If they see something is not working, they do something about it. That needs to be your attitude as our world and economy goes through yet another era.

We are living in exciting times of change, be sure you are taking advantage of every opportunity and hustle while you have the energy.

Rich and Free Entrepreneur's Guide

- An entrepreneur is a gain seeker, not simply a risk taker.
- You're allowed to have more than one source of income, count on it.
- You have your own identity, you are not your job.
- Entrepreneurs are thinking 24/7, Day jobs are 9-5.
- Hustle while you're young.
- The successful are having fun creating wealth and so should you.

Chapter 15

Don't Quit That Job: How to Get Rich While Working for Others

You only get out of it what you put into it. If you are a sheep in this world, you're not going to get much out of it.
—**Greg Norman**
"The Great White Shark"
Australian Golfer and Entrepreneur

Money does not make you rich; your skills make you rich. Over time, your skills appreciate and what you learn is leverage. The job may go away but not the knowledge you have gained. Things change over time, keep up with what is happening. Your career is leveraged by your education.

People want growth and development in a career. The future of a job is continuing education. With career development, you can better ensure a future that will be enjoyable and rewarding.

Many people have jobs they enjoy; their careers are working for them. They don't want the responsibility or risk of being an entrepreneur or starting a business. They just want to reach their full potential working for others.

The problem is getting rich and wealthy will not happen to you just because you have a good job or you have a good education. Even if you follow the rules, working for others will only give you income and job satisfaction.

> **It Is Not Your Boss's Job To Make You Rich; Their Job Is To Keep You Working For Wages.**

A career is only as good as the people and managers you work for and the health of the company. At any point and at any time, be prepared to have your skills and knowledge transferred to a new job or career. No job is guaranteed.

Companies are sold, go broke, merge, and change. Anyone of these things can happen to you no matter how hard you work or how important your contribution. Being realistic about chance and change has nothing to do with reaching goals and maximizing your potential.

The better you do at your job, and the more you keep up your skills, knowledge, and education, the easier it is to transfer skills to new companies and opportunities.

Entitlement Thinking Is Dangerous

The better your education, talents and abilities, the better job you can land. However, once you get a job or are

Don't Quit That Job   191

in a career, the career game changes and becomes, "Show Me!"

Advantages that got you in the door go right out the window without performance. If the people you work with feel your attitude is entitlement because you're smart, have an advanced degree, or a high IQ, you could be short lived. Business in the 21st Century is far more competitive and fast track than the last generation.

The way to gain success at work is be in tune with the new working conditions. To gain all the opportunity within your reach, understand the company's vision as well as your own.

Company Problems Are Opportunity

Just like the entrepreneur, see change as opportunity, not a threat. The bad news for companies may be your good news and opportunity. Companies deal with faster, smarter, and more aggressive competition than at any time in our history. We have more competitors from different cultures competing in the same arena.

The measurement of an employee today is against not only your city and your state, but the world. Companies no longer have an advantage because of fast computers and brilliant software. Everyone has that capability.

The key to success is in your thinking! If you bring innovation and creativity to your job and career, you will be adding value. If competitors have the brightest people, it can only be matched with brains and thinking.

I know I was not the sharpest blade in the drawer when I started my career. My experience was limited but I kept trying to think how I could do things better. I was not afraid of being different.

My imagination and creativity were well beyond my IQ and intelligence; I was able to think my way to success. People are more capable and creative than given credit for. Adversity helped me become self sufficient and willing go to out on my own. Everyone is more enlightened because of education, television, computers, the media, and the internet.

> **The Biggest Single Advantage You Have In A Career Is You Can Think. Companies Need Thinkers!**

I went from selling brushes in high school to running companies on my ability to use my brains, and my brains are average. What was not average was my confidence and creativity.

Companies that do not pay attention to how fast things are moving and how stiff the competition is will be gone. If you are working for one of those companies, do not waste your time. Get with a winner.

You need to be in the right environment to be a winner. It does not do any good to be the best deck chair arranger if your ship is the RMS Titanic. If you help the team and show them opportunity, in time, you will be leading the team.

> **The Secret To Reaching Full Potential In A Career Is To Work And Think Like An Entrepreneur.**

We have more people with more education and ability competing for top paying jobs than ever before. Yet companies are in desperate need to find workers who will do more than just what they are told to do.

To be successful you, be a good communicator and you will be able to influence others, sell yourself and your ideas. If you cannot sell yourself and your ideas, it is not likely you will get the opportunity to manage others and gain responsibility. With responsibility comes authority. With authority comes power.

In business and in your career, it takes power to get ahead. Being a brand helps your income and security. Be a performing standout.

The skills of entrepreneurs are also the skills of performers in any business. However, you are only earning income and it is highly unlikely you have any equity in the company. To get rich and wealthy while you are working for others, do more than be successful at the job. Become a success while *you are not on the job.*

How to Get Rich on the Job

A job may not make you rich but a good job will give you income, a sense of well being and contribution.

> **It's What You Do In Your Spare Time That Makes You Rich.**

It's old news about the last generation, lifelong jobs, careers, pensions and one family income. Today you can get rich and wealthy by using your job as leverage to do more. The long-term plan to wealth is to create enough assets that will take care of you and give you cash flow to live and not have to work.

The thought of retirement is great until people discover retirement is highly overrated. Many find out it was more fun working, having something to do and the extra spending money made things even more enjoyable.

Many outrageously wealthy people could retire and live like royalty, but work makes them happy. Business keeps you young, sharp, and alert. It may be a better idea to *grow into a retiring job* or start a new career late in life than sitting on a beach watching seagulls.

Before you charge out and do anything with your finances, learn the language and vocabulary about saving plans. Be sure you meet people who are advising you for your personal interest and not selling you anything. You do not want to get advice from people who have a conflict of interest. Read, learn, and pay for advice that will help you, not make someone else rich selling you things.

As an employee, you do not have that many options compared to a business owner or the self-employed. However, the choices you do have are good and easy enough to accomplish.

> **You Create Long-Term
> Wealth With Compound Interest.**

The younger you are when starting, the more the interest compounds over the years. Save and invest smart and make it a habit. Saving needs to be a relentless effort every month. It is not rocket science. It's just simple math.

Over a lifetime of working, you can accumulate much more than most imagine. Time is your best guarantee that you will reach your goals and be a winner. You can make millions even if you have a modest job and earn average income. Pay yourself first and save before you spend your money on anything else.

401K-The Modern Day Pension

A 401k is a retirement plan that allows eligible employees of a company to save and invest for their own retirement on a tax-deferred basis. Only an employer is allowed to sponsor a 401k for their employees. You decide how much money you want deducted from your paycheck and deposited to the plan based on limits imposed by the plans provisions and IRS rules. Your employer may also choose to contribute to the plan, but this is optional. Even if your employer does not contribute to your plan, you are still deferring taxes. You do not owe income taxes on the money contributed until you withdraw it from the plan.

If you leave the company, you have options with a 401K Plan. Your choices are to leave your money in your company's plan, roll over your 401(k) into your next employer's 401k or a rollover IRA, or take a distribution. The advantages of a rollover are that your money continues to grow tax-deferred and that you may have more investment choices. Later, you can put it into a new employer's plan if it remains separate from other IRA funds. Keeping your funds with your former employer reduces the hassle for you and may preserve your ability to borrow from your retirement plan. Taking a distribution may be tempting, but if you are under 59 ½ you may incur penalties and have taxes withheld. If you take money out you will potentially miss the years of tax-deferred compounding and that is the secret to creating wealth in long-term savings accounts.

Open an IRA

Outside of a corporate retirement plan, an IRA is the great way to accumulate tax-advantaged savings. With a Roth IRA, you contribute after tax dollars but it accumulates tax-free growth. The Traditional IRA is tax deductible up front but you pay taxes at the rate of your income when you retire and start to withdraw your money and it may be lower than your current tax rate. IRAs are limited to how much you can contribute. (Currently, in 2007, the limit is a modest $4,000.) That has nothing to do with the fact that an IRA is a big winner over time. If you start either a Roth or traditional IRA at 23 years old, use a 6% rate of return, contribute every year, you will have accumulated about $500,000 by the time you are 59.5. The power of compounding interest over time is hard to beat.

Don't Stop, Do More

Saving in 401Ks and IRAs are great but why stop? Why not do more? In the old days, it might not have been necessary. Today, it is mandatory.

To balance your income, look to have something that YOU OWN. Savings is an extension of your job; it is simply taking what you earn and putting a portion away. Owning something that generates cash flow is different.

A business you and your family can manage while you work a job is leverage. Use OPM! If you were to buy a rental house and put a small down payment and the rent covered the mortgage payment, over time, the rent would pay off the house for you. You need to maintain the house but the cost of the house is using the leverage of OPM, others are paying off your retirement investments. One of the reasons real estate is so popular is that it allows tax advantages far better than a job does.

A business sold and another one bought may fall under the Starker 1031 tax-deferred exchange rules. You need a professional to show you how to do this but it's common long-term strategy that will compound your money while you work and earn income at a job. With real estate investing, you can defer taxes and build an empire while others are paying off your mortgage.

The government bends over backwards to help entrepreneurs and business people because they create jobs and more jobs means more taxpayers. Invest in things that give you lower capital tax gains and advantages. You earn more and you can keep more.

Use your brains, sell, and market yourself or you will be swimming in a sea of competition from new college graduates entering the work force. Go to work but think and act like an entrepreneur.

If you work at your job and you put in the same amount of effort for your own personal gains, over 30 years of work, you can easily make millions of dollars.

Use the good kind of debt to create wealth-creating leverage. Use other people's money to acquire assets that grow over time.

The combination of work and smart strategies make you rich. Be patient and think long term.

Learn financial literacy. Getting rich at a job while working for others is a two-track system. Even the simplest plan of buying a small home every two years using a modest down payment means that in 20 years you would have 10 homes. In 30 years, you should have enough cash flow to live on and that may be the starting point, not the end of the game.

The real fun starts when you have capital gains and tax deferred money to play with, you can make even more money. That is how the rich do it. The rich spend money from their cash flow to buy more assets that go up in value. Do as the rich do and it's a matter of time until you join the ranks of the rich and wealthy.

Rich and Free Entrepreneur's Guide

- Your skills make you rich.
- What you do in your spare time is what will make you rich and wealthy.
- Go to work and be your best.
- The secret to wealth while working for others is the compound interest of your savings and investments.
- Be a diligent saver and investor, your job is only current income.
- Creating wealth is a marathon, start saving early.

Thanks for Reading!

I hope this book gives you ideas and helps get you started if you have not done so already. Times are extraordinary, look for opportunity, think like an entrepreneur.

Working your way up in a career is competitive because there are so many competing for the good paying jobs. Yet companies are desperate for smart, creative, and innovative people.

Few are willing to step out, take the risk, and do more and that is the key. If you do work for others, be the best or you will find yourself simply, another worker and a commodity.

If you do not like your job or you are just unhappy with what you are doing, this is the best time in history to be an entrepreneur. Discover for yourself that we truly are living in the land of opportunity.

I wish you the best of luck,
Brian J. Bieler

About the Author

Brian J. Bieler

Brian J. Bieler has more than thirty years of business, managing, marketing, and sales experience. He began his career selling copy paper and by the age of twenty-four was a sales supervisor in midtown Manhattan.

Brian then went into the advertising business at *Women's Wear Daily* and *Mademoiselle Magazine* in New York City. Later he joined Sudbrink Broadcasting, a leading-edge radio group specializing in buying and improving underperforming companies.

Brian became an accomplished executive in local, regional, and national broadcasting. He was Vice President and General Manager of ten major market radio stations from coast to coast and President of the Viacom Radio Group in New York City, produced workshops with Excellerated Business Schools and was President of Westworks Marketing.

Brian is an author, entrepreneur, and speaker.

To Order Books

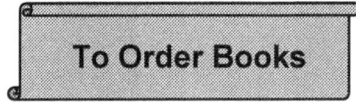

Telephone Orders: 1-800-980-5099

Email Book Orders or contact: richandfree@cox.net

Postal Orders:
   Little Falls Press
   7000 North 16th Street, Suite 120 #489
   Phoenix, AZ, 85020

Please send (number of copies_____) *Rich and Free* to:

Name (please print):_____

Address:_____

City:_____State:_____Zip:_____

Country:_____

Telephone:_____

Email address:_____

$17.95 U.S. Dollars per book.

Arizona residents please add local sales tax.

U. S. Shipping and Handling add $4.00 per book and $2.00 for each additional book in same shipment.

International Shipping and handling add $8.00 per book and $5.00 for each additional book in same shipment.

Payment: Cheque: ☐   Credit Card: ☐

Visa: ☐   Master Card: ☐   AMEX: ☐   Discover: ☐

Card Number:_____

Name On Card:_____

Expiration Date On Card:_____

Visit our web site
www.richandfreeguide.com

www.ingramcontent.com/pod-product-compliance
Lightning Source LLC
Chambersburg PA
CBHW031931190326
41519CB00007B/490